Quick Start Drawing

PEOPLE

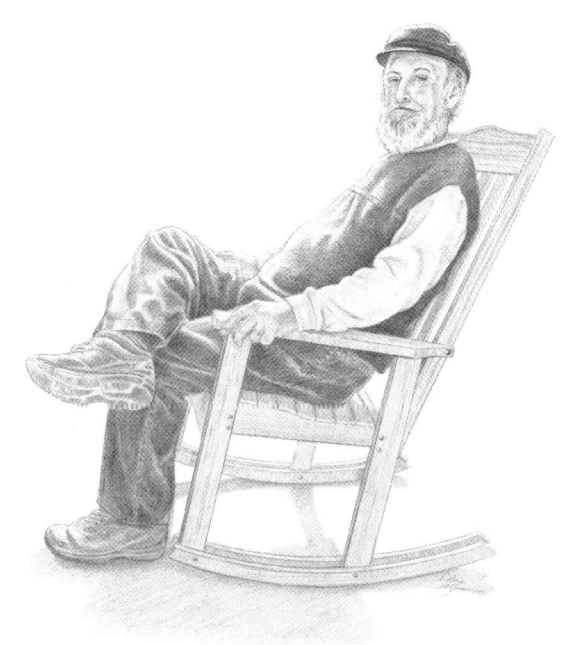

Walter Foster

About This Book

Welcome to *Quick Start Drawing People.* Packed with dozens of drawing prompts, helpful techniques, step-by-step lessons, and easy tracing exercises, this drawing pad is ideal for beginning and aspiring artists who enjoy learning by doing. As such, you will build basic art knowledge and drawing skills in a short time, while learning to create your own unique artwork along the way.

After learning more about the tools of the trade, you will discover basic skills, including how to hold the pencil and how to draw basic strokes. From there, you'll learn to draw basic shapes and develop them with shading, and then you'll learn to hone your skills through dozens of drawing tutorials focused on the human form, including head position, facial features, perspective, movement, and more. The art in this drawing pad is designed to be enhanced by you, so we've also included unfinished drawings printed in light gray to use as a foundation on which to build your skills. It's the perfect starting point for beginners. High-quality paper means you can draw inside without worrying about the pages underneath, so be brave and experiment! We recommend keeping a sketchbook or sketch pad in addition to this drawing pad so that you can continue to practice the featured lessons.

Getting Started

Drawing doesn't require a lot of materials. A good HB pencil and this drawing pad are perfect for getting started. The next few pages go over the fundamentals of drawing, including some basic tools, how to hold and sharpen a pencil, and how to create a variety of basic strokes. A good drawing features an interplay between light and dark, so you will learn a bit about shading techniques and creating a value scale. Throughout this pad, look for step-by-step projects to help guide you through the drawing process. Let's get started!

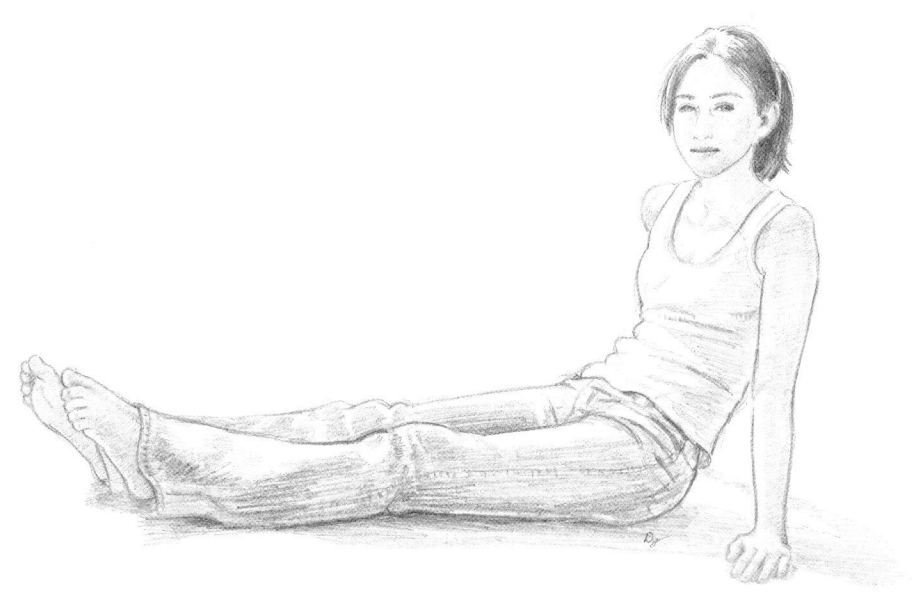

Tools and Materials

Pencils are classified according to the hardness of the lead. H leads are hard and perfect for light, sketchy strokes. B leads are soft and better for darker lines. HB leads are in between H and B; these pencils are incredibly versatile. Start with an H pencil and an HB pencil. Make sure you have a standard pencil sharpener on hand as well as an artist's knife for more precise sharpening. You will also need erasers and extra drawing paper for practicing. As your skills improve, you can expand your artist's tool kit.

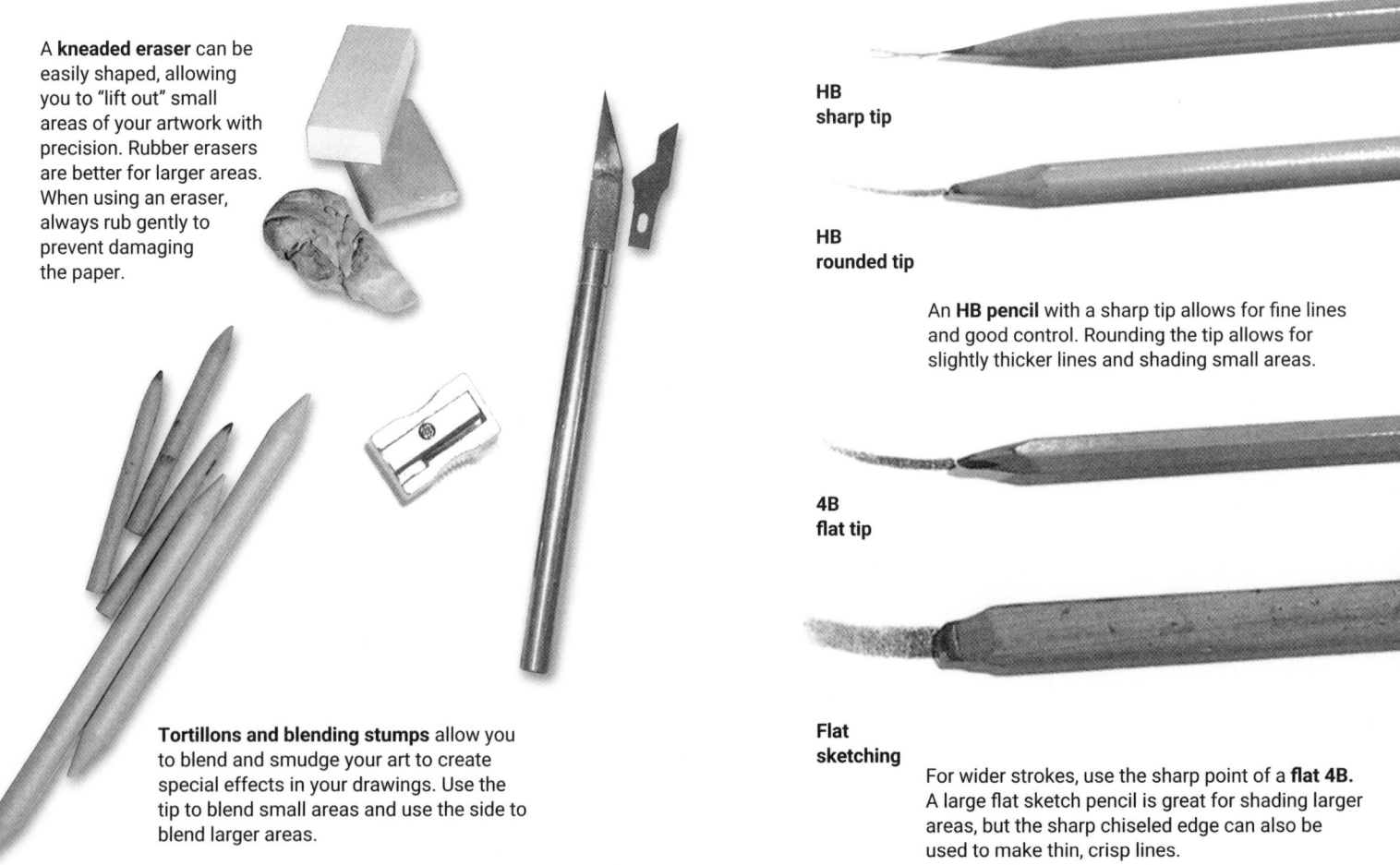

A **kneaded eraser** can be easily shaped, allowing you to "lift out" small areas of your artwork with precision. Rubber erasers are better for larger areas. When using an eraser, always rub gently to prevent damaging the paper.

Tortillons and blending stumps allow you to blend and smudge your art to create special effects in your drawings. Use the tip to blend small areas and use the side to blend larger areas.

HB sharp tip

HB rounded tip

An **HB pencil** with a sharp tip allows for fine lines and good control. Rounding the tip allows for slightly thicker lines and shading small areas.

4B flat tip

Flat sketching

For wider strokes, use the sharp point of a **flat 4B**. A large flat sketch pencil is great for shading larger areas, but the sharp chiseled edge can also be used to make thin, crisp lines.

Sharpening Pencils

There are many ways to sharpen your drawing pencils outside of using a standard handheld sharpener. Try each of the methods below to see which one you prefer.

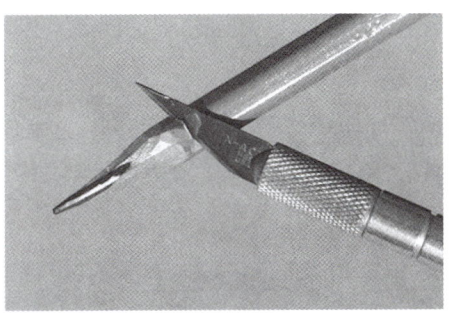

Artist knives are ideal for shaping pencils in specific ways to give them a chisel-shaped, blunt, or flat tip. Hold the knife at an angle to the pencil and carve away from the body. Always cut only a small amount of the lead and wood.

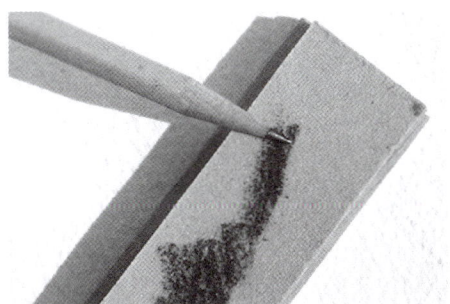

Use a **sandpaper block** to quickly shape a lead. Sandpaper also removes some of the wood coating. The finer the grit, the better you can control the result. You'll need to roll the pencil in your hand while sharpening to ensure the lead sharpens evenly.

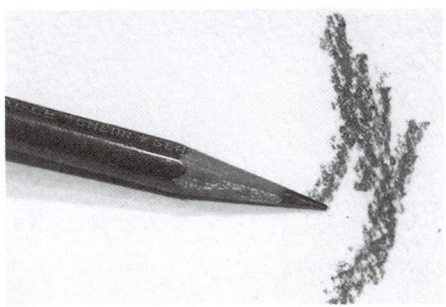

Rough paper is ideal for smoothing a lead that you've sharpened with sandpaper. This is a great way to create a fine point for tiny details. Gently rotate the pencil to sharpen the lead evenly.

Holding the Pencil

There are different ways to hold a pencil, each of which has its own purpose. When drawing, use the strength and dexterity of your entire arm to prevent your wrist and fingers from cramping or getting too tight. Try to maintain a relaxed position and hold the pencil lightly.

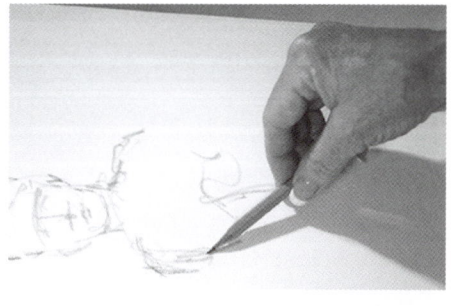

Basic Underhand This technique allows your arm and wrist to move freely, which results in fresh, lively sketches. Drawing in this position makes it easy to use both the point and the side of the pencil lead.

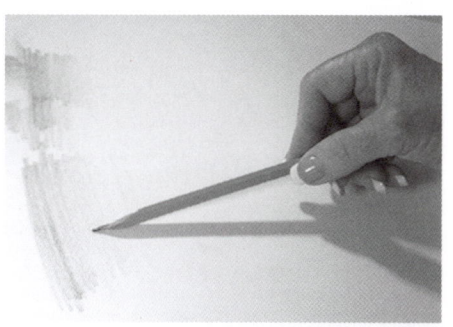

Underhand Variation Holding the pencil at its end enables you to make long and short light strokes. It also gives you control over lights, darks, and textures. It can help to place a protective sheet of paper under your hand so you don't smudge your drawing.

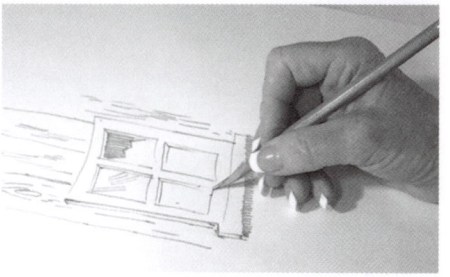

Writing The writing position is the most common, and it provides the most control for precise lines and fine details. Be careful not to press on your drawing too hard or grip the pencil too tightly.

Draw a few lines and squiggles using the three different pencil-holding techniques shown on the previous page. How does each grip change your drawing?

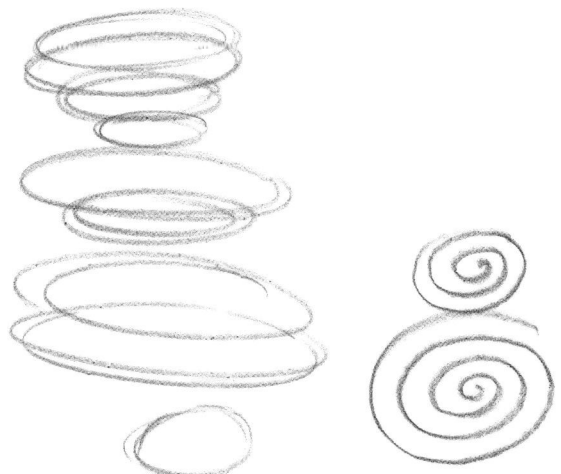

Basic Techniques

When learning to draw, it's helpful to try out a variety of drawing pencils to observe how the lines you draw change with each pencil. Finely detailed drawings are best rendered with a sharpened pencil, held in the writing position. Larger areas of a drawing are easier to shade with the flat side of a pencil held from your wrist. Be curious and try each hand position with different pencils. You'll be excited by the different results!

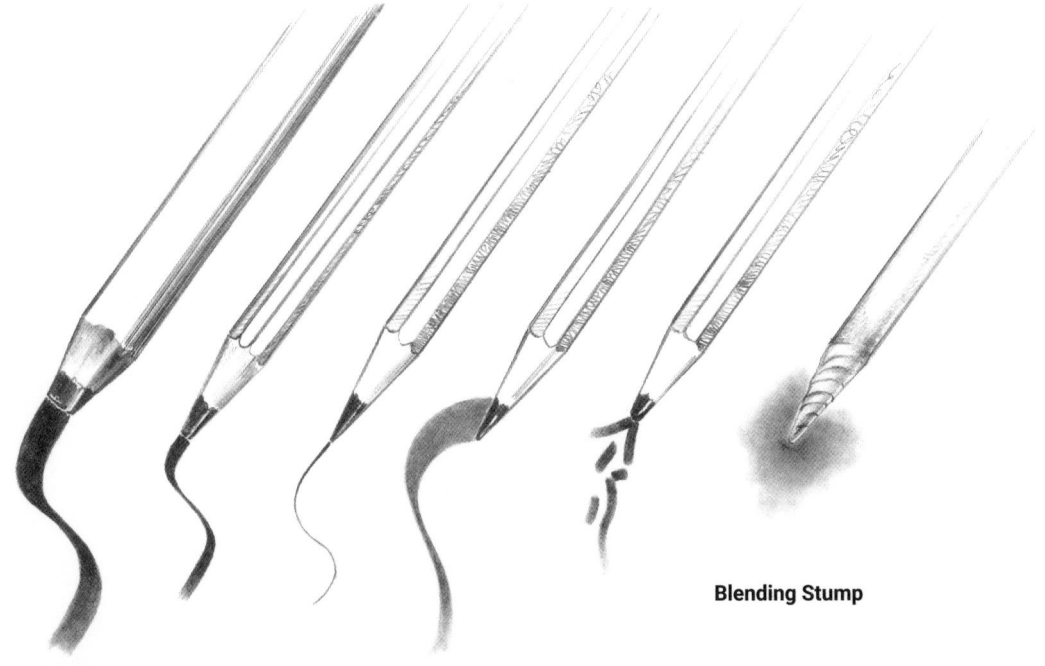

Blending Stump

Flat Tip   **Chiseled Tip**   **Pointed Tip**   **Rounded Tip**   **Blunt Tip**

Practicing basic techniques will help you understand how to manipulate the pencil to acheive a variety of effects. Practice the techniques shown below in the areas provided.

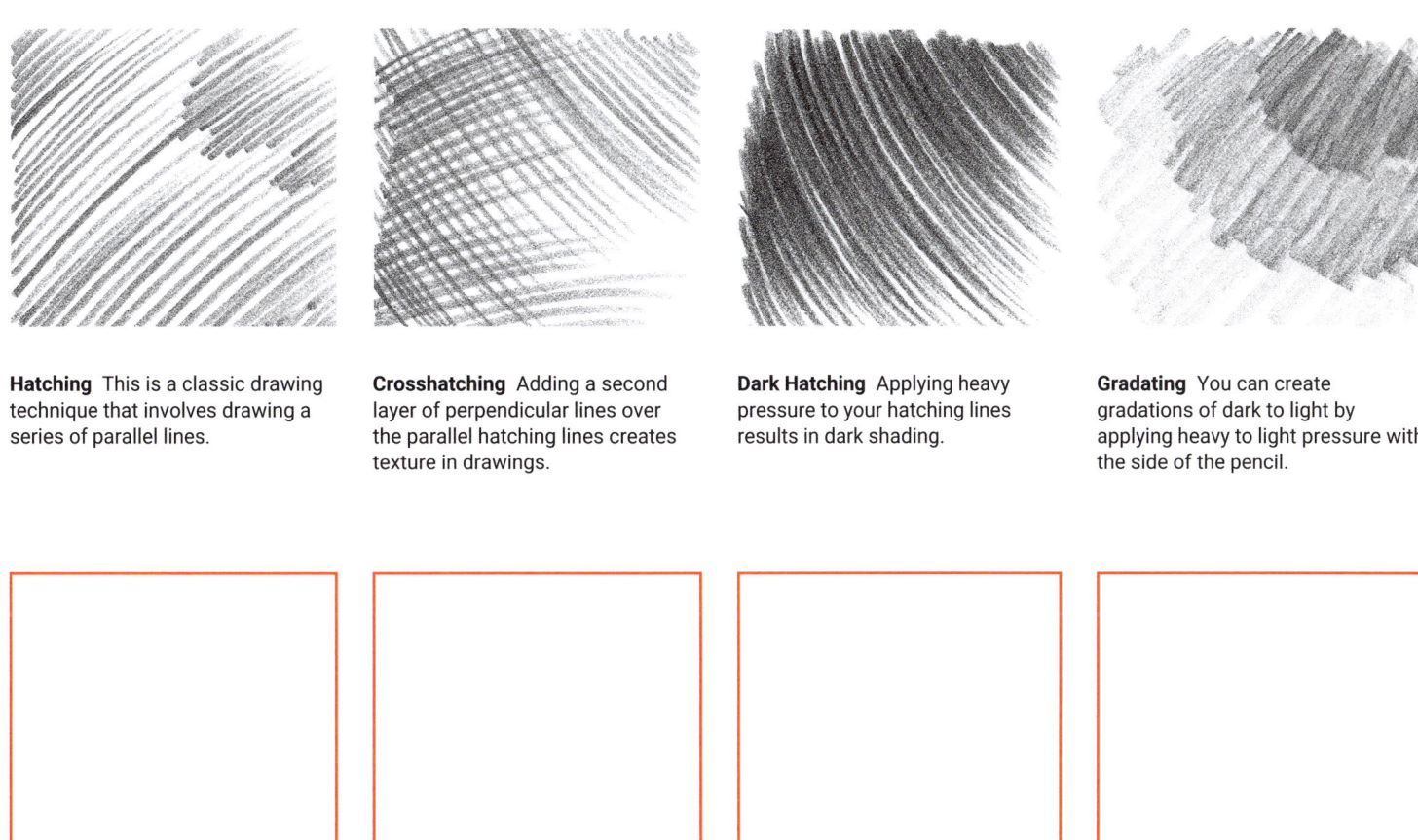

Hatching This is a classic drawing technique that involves drawing a series of parallel lines.

Crosshatching Adding a second layer of perpendicular lines over the parallel hatching lines creates texture in drawings.

Dark Hatching Applying heavy pressure to your hatching lines results in dark shading.

Gradating You can create gradations of dark to light by applying heavy to light pressure with the side of the pencil.

Seeing Values

Value is the basic term used to describe the relative lightness or darkness of a color. In pencil drawing, the values range from white to grays to black, and it's the variation among lights and darks (made with shading) and the range of values in shadows and highlights that give a two-dimensional drawing a three-dimensional look. This value scale shows the gradation from black, the darkest value, through various shades of gray and ending with the lightest value.

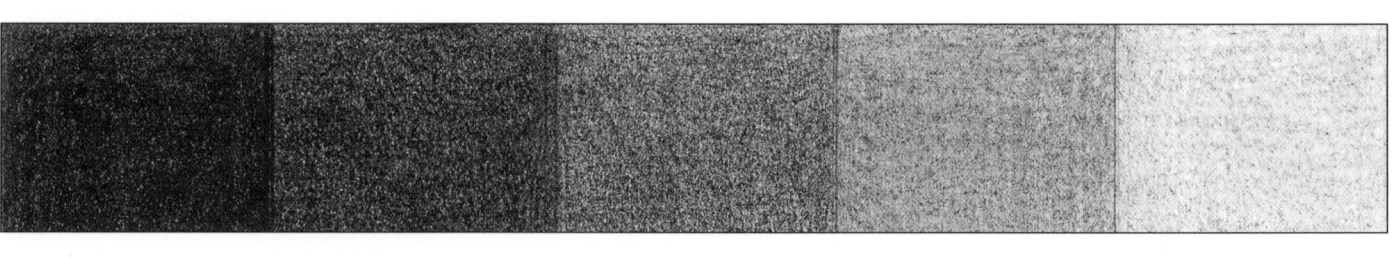

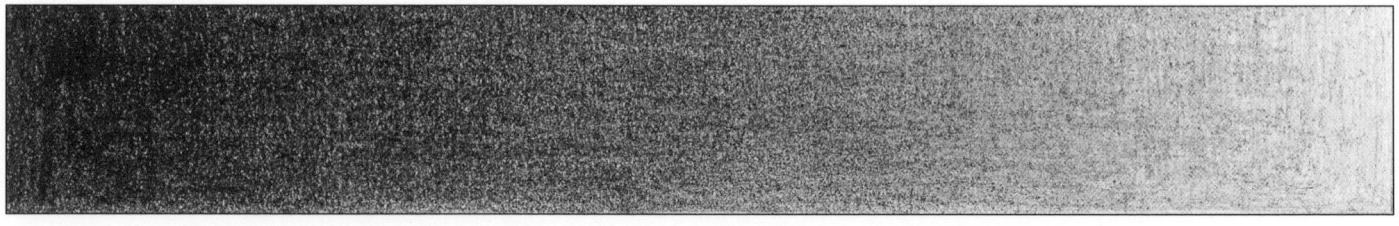

Create your own value scales in the areas below. Use an HB pencil to create one value scale. Then use pencils of varying hardness (2B, HB, and H) to create another value scale. Compare how the different pencils create different effects.

Basic Shapes

Anyone can draw just about anything by simply breaking down the subject into a few basic shapes: circles, rectangles, squares, and triangles. By drawing an outline around the basic shapes of your subject, you have drawn its shape. But your subject also has depth and dimension, or form. The corresponding forms of the basic shapes are spheres, cylinders, cubes, and cones. Sketching the shapes and developing their forms is the first step of every drawing. After that, it's essentially just connecting and refining the lines and adding details.

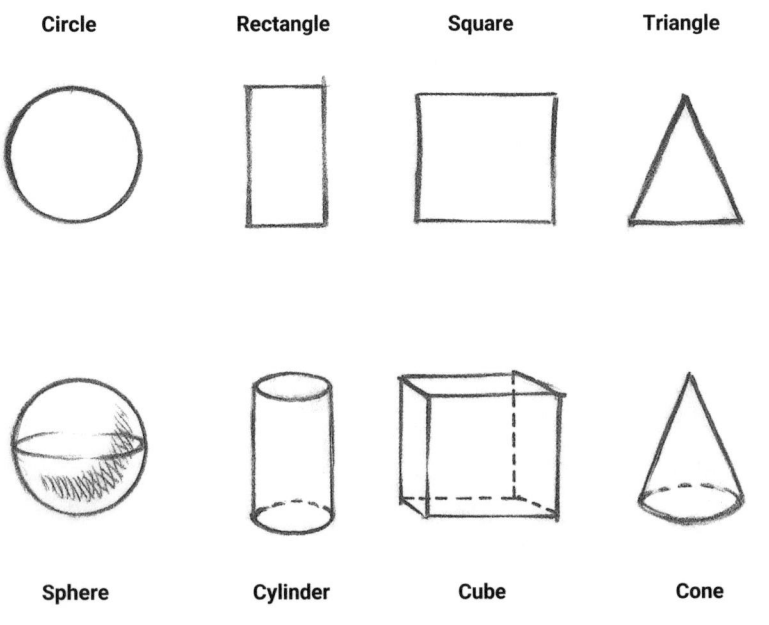

These diagrams show to how to draw the forms of these four basic shapes. The ellipses show the backs of the circle, cynlinder, and cone, and the cube is drawn by connecting two squares with parallel lines.

Building Form

Once you've established the general shape and form of the subject using basic shapes, refine your drawing by applying value through hatching, crosshatching, and gradating. Gather some objects from around your home or continue to practice using basic shapes.

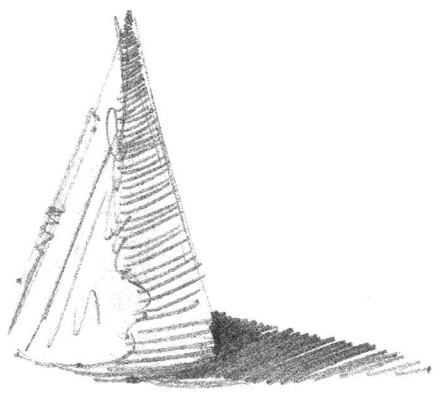

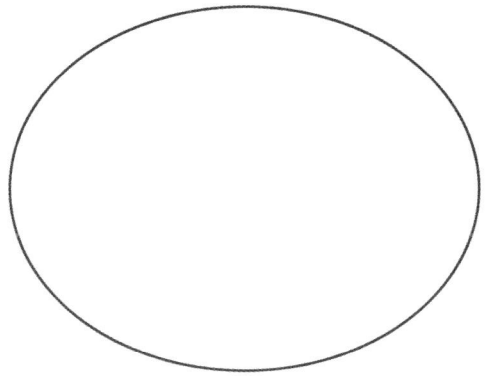

Outline

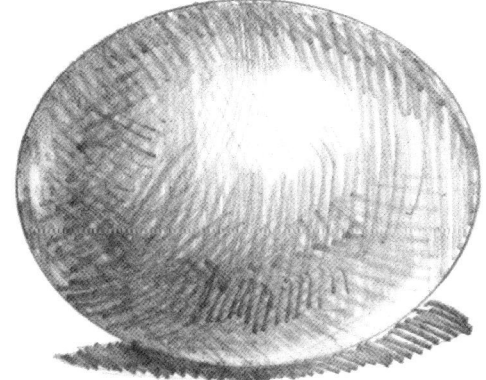

with Depth

The secret to transforming an outline into a form is proper shading. Use less pressure for lighter areas and more pressure for darker areas. When hatching, consider where the light is coming from. Where it falls directly onto the object, a light reflection is created, creating the brightest area. Also consider the cast shadow, which is the shadow cast by your object. Directly above the darkest part of the cast shadow, the object is very light—like the egg shown here.

Contour Drawing

Contour drawing is helpful for training your hand to draw lines exactly as you see them. Pick a starting point on your subject, and then draw only the contours—or outlines—of the shapes. Don't look at your paper, but allow your hands to do the work, drawing the lines exactly as your eye sees them.

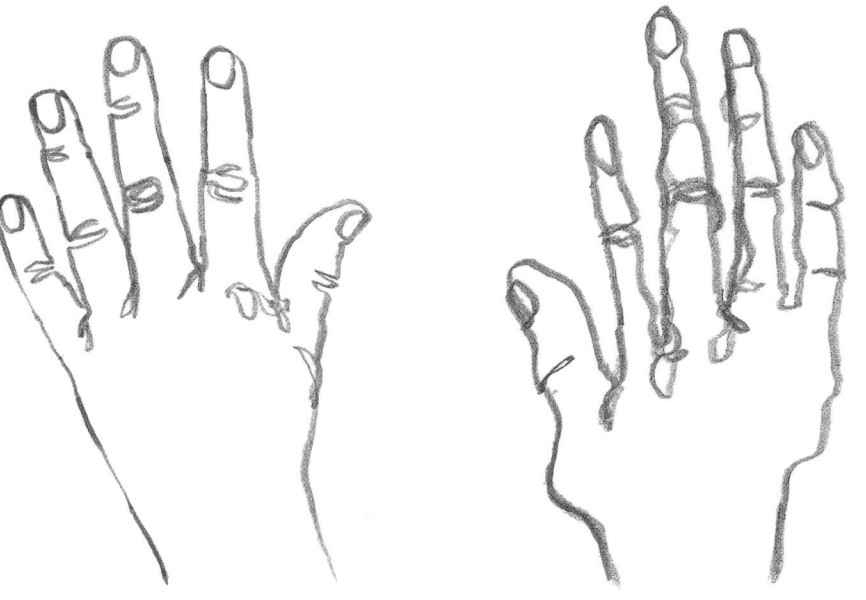

Drawing "Blind" This contour drawing can be made while occasionally looking down at the paper while you draw your hand. The second drawing, above right, is an example of a blind contour drawing in which you draw without looking at your paper. Blind contour drawing is one of the best ways to learn to draw only what you see.

Try to create a blind contour drawing of your own hand without looking at the paper as you draw.

Continous Line Drawing

Trace this subject using one continuous line. Then try it again on your own, concentrating on the subject and tracing the outlines you see. Instead of lifting your pencil between shapes, keep the line unbroken by freely looping back and crossing over your lines.

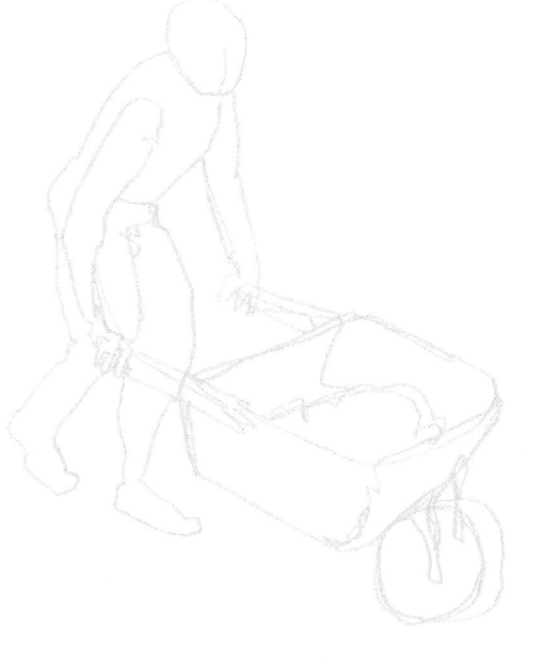

Repeat the previous exercise using the subjects below.

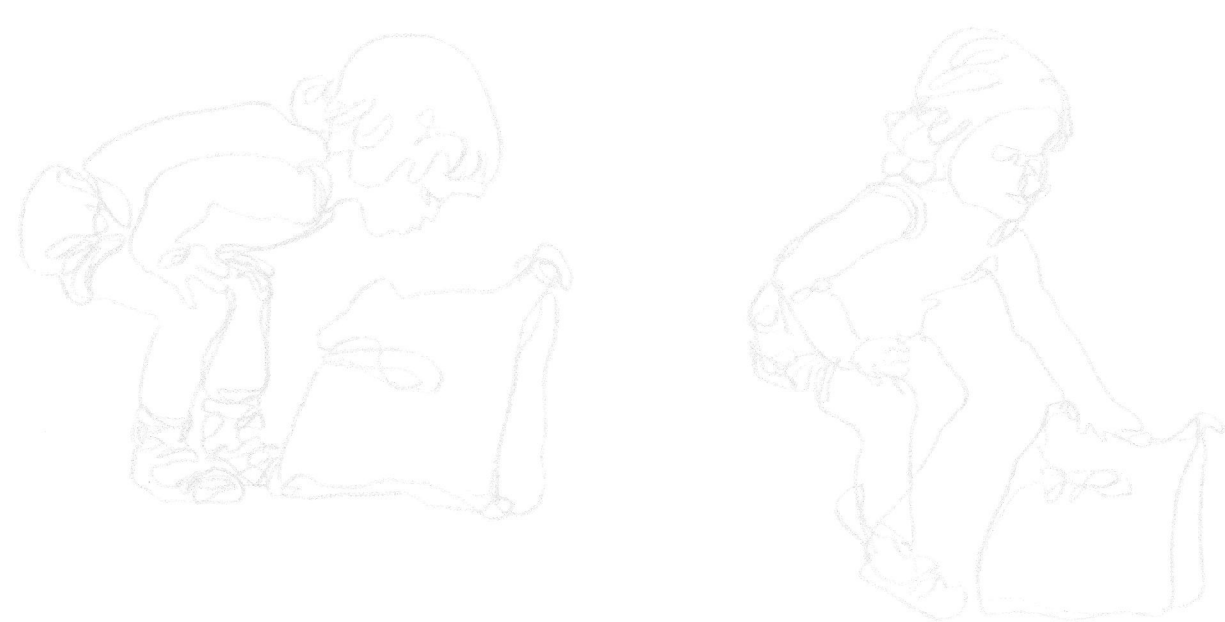

Facial Contours

Drawing contours and analyzing surfaces are important for developing a better understanding of head shape. Remember to look at the model and not at your paper while you draw. This makes it easier to recognize and depict the subtleties of the contours.

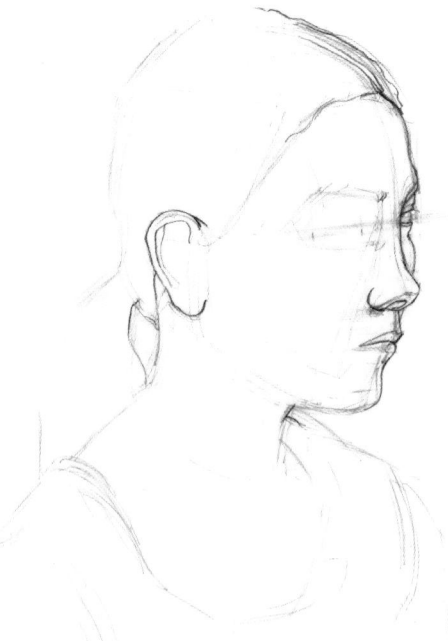

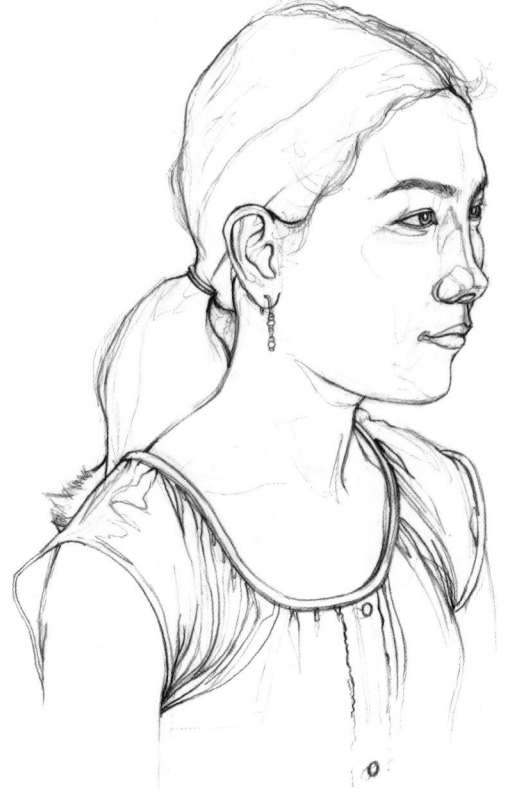

2 Emphasize various elements using different line thicknesses. Indicate hair and other intricate details with delicate strokes.

1 Sketch the subject with light strokes. Draw guidelines for the eyes and other features.Capture the overall shape of the head and shoulders

Trace the outlines with a soft pencil and add shading to emphasize the areas of light and shadow.

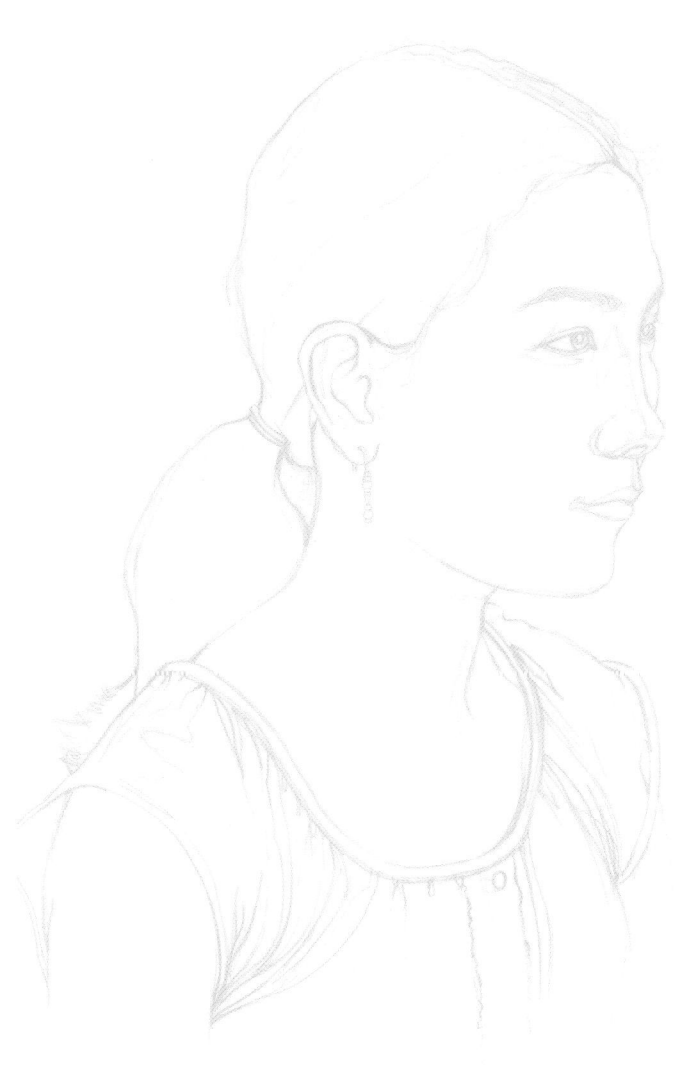

Head and Face

The boxes shown here correlate with the head positions directly below them. When starting out, drawing boxes like these will help you correctly position the head. The boxes also allow the major frontal and profile planes, or level surfaces, of the face to be discernable. Once you become comfortable with this process, practice drawing the heads shown on this page.

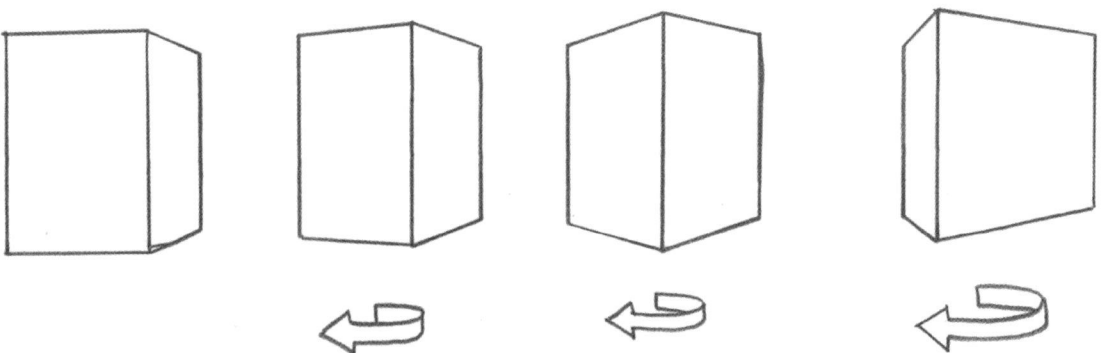

When drawing, pay attention to rules of perspective on the small space you are using.

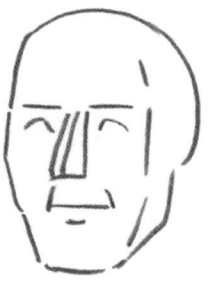
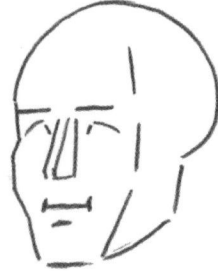
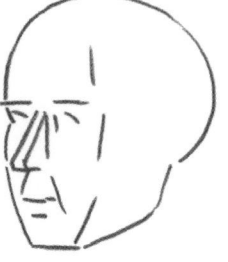
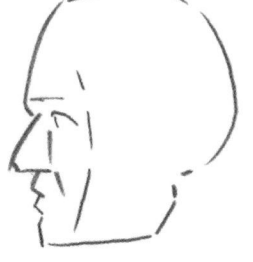

With just a few strokes, the rough shape of a smiling face starts to take form.
Place strokes with care following the rules of perspective.

Try drawing basic heads and faces inside these boxes, using the rules of perspective. Once you are comfortable working inside the boxes, try drawing underneath without the guidelines.

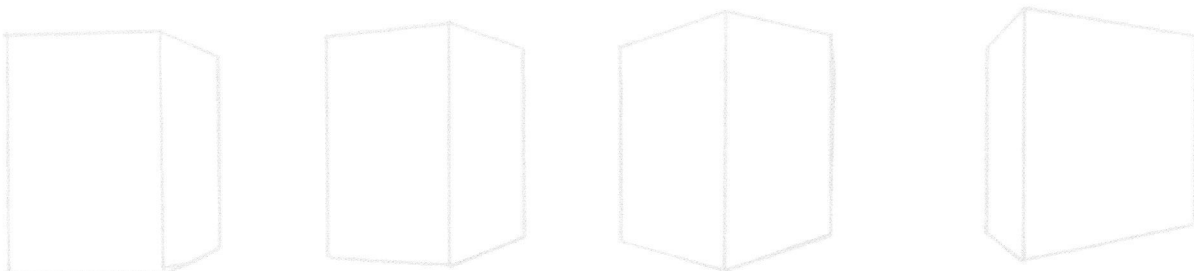

Views of the Head

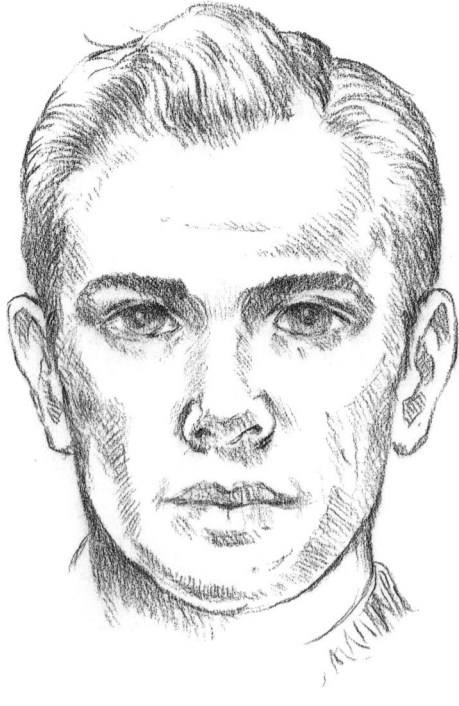

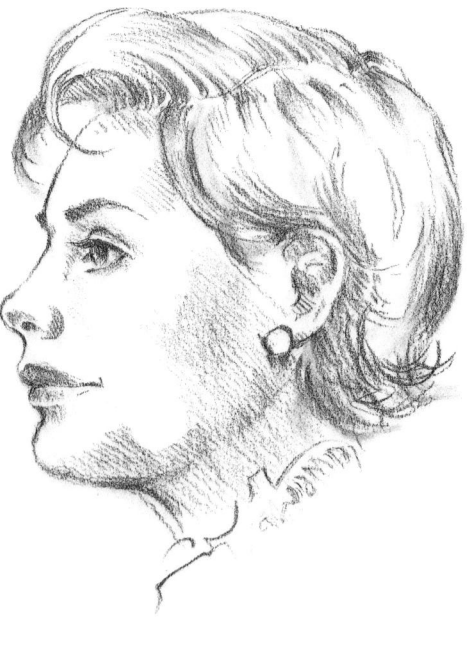

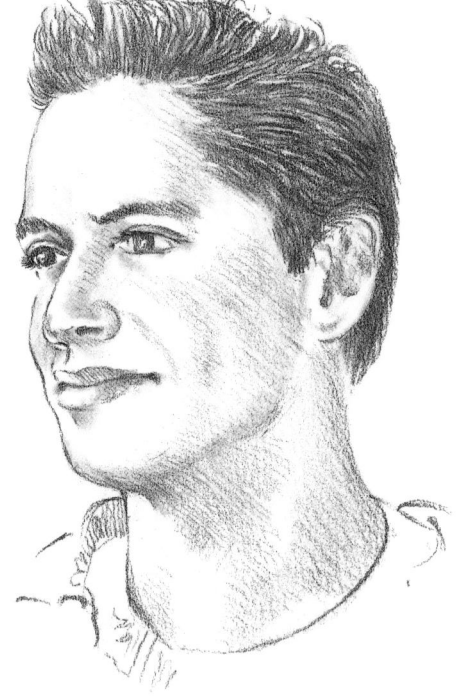

Frontal View In a frontal view, we can see that the face is not perfectly symmetrical. One eye is generally smaller than the other, or one might sit at a slightly different angle. The same is true of the ears, cheeks, and the sides of the nose and mouth.

Profile The head shape changes in a side view, but the features remain in the same relative positions. Although the nose is a prominent feature in a profile, take care not to let it dominate the face. Also, pay attention to where the eye sits and how the lower lip curves into the chin.

Three-Quarter View This view can be challenging because the features are positioned at an angle. Start with a contour drawing to work out how the features really look and then develop the details.

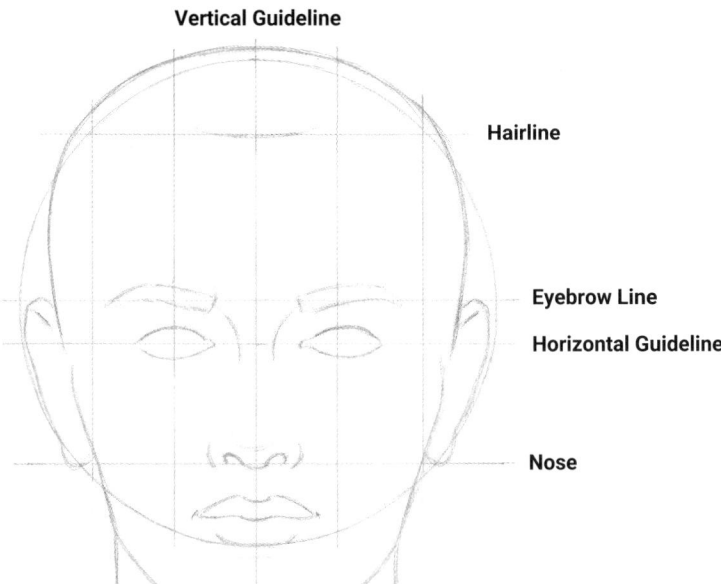

Vertical Guideline

Hairline

Eyebrow Line

Horizontal Guideline

Nose

Front View Visualize the head as a flattened ball. Divide the ball in half horizontally and vertically, and then divide the face horizontally into three equal parts: the hairline, the eyebrow line, and the nose line. Use these guidelines to determine the correct placement and spacing of the facial features.

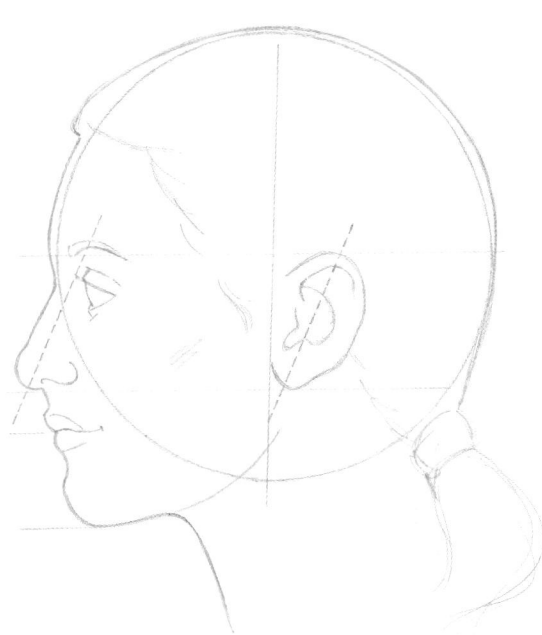

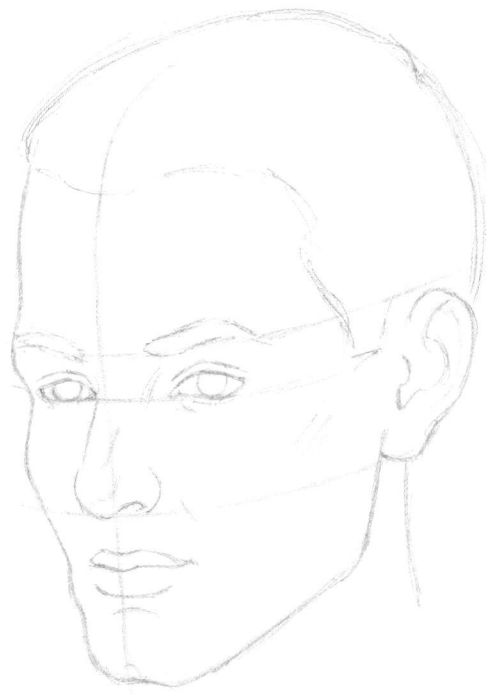

Side View Use the large cranial circle as a guideline for placing the features. The nose, lips, and chin fall outside the circle, whereas the eyes and ear remain inside. The slanted, broken lines indicate the parallel slant of the nose and ear.

Three-Quarter View When the head turns, the eye closest to the viewer (in this case, the left eye) appears larger than the other eye. This is a technique called "foreshortening," in which elements of a drawing are distorted to create the illusion of three-dimensional space; objects closer to the viewer appear larger than objects that are farther away.

Placing Features

Learning proper head proportions will help you render faces accurately. Review the measurements and guidelines in the illustration below. Notice how the basic head shape is oval.

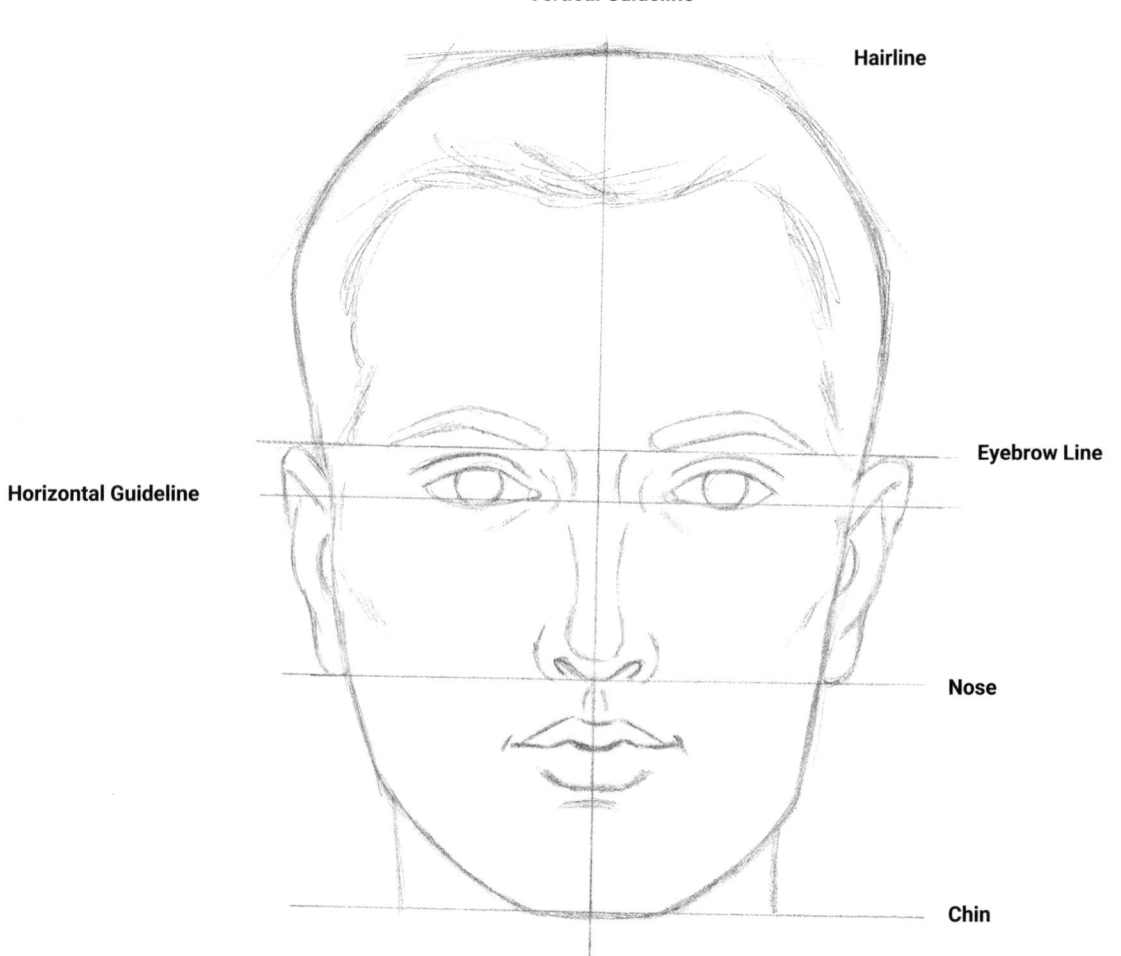

The eyes are positioned exactly between the horizontal guideline and the eyebrow line. The tip of the nose is midway between the eyebrow line and the chin line. The lower lip ends midway between the nose and chin. The ears extend from the eyebrow line to the tip of the nose.

Practice mastering proportions by completing the face below.

Facial Planes

Once you understand the basic structure of the head, you can simplify the complex shapes of the skull into geometric planes. These planes are the foundation for shading; they act as a guide to help you properly place highlights and shadows.

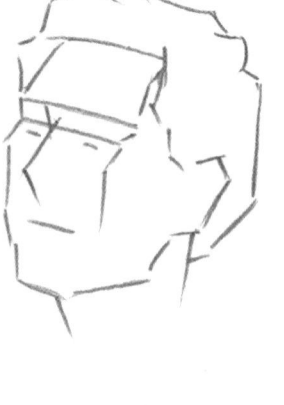

1 Keep guidelines light so they won't show in your actual drawing.

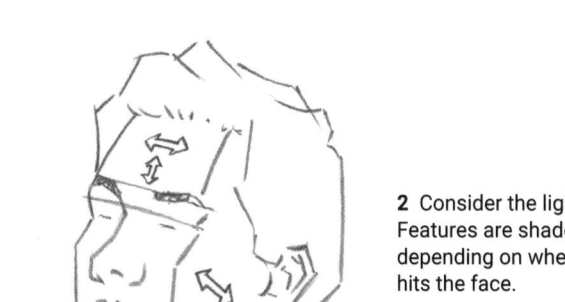
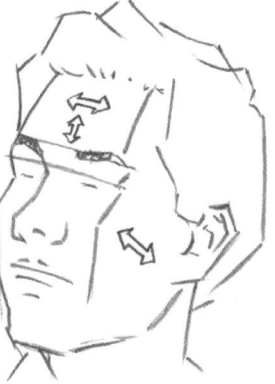

2 Consider the light source. Features are shaded differently depending on where the light hits the face.

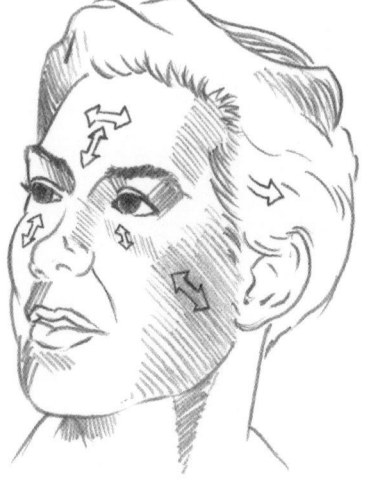

3 Your shading strokes should follow the arrow directions to bring out the contours of the face.

Use the guidelines below to practice drawing
the head in a three-quarter view.

Drawing Eyes

Eyes are an important element of any portrait, and they're surprisingly easy to draw once you know how. Practice drawing eyes following the steps below.

Front View

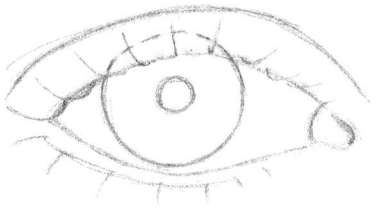

1 First, draw the circle for the iris; then place the crescent-shaped eyelid over it. Draw the lower eyelid, lashes, and the corner of the eye.

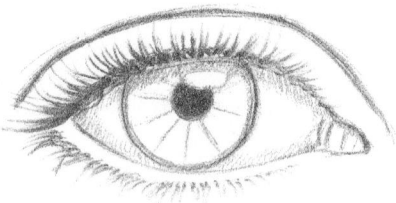

2 Now draw "rays" pointing outward from the pupil. Fill in the eyelashes and the upper eyelid as well as the black pupil and the reflection of light.

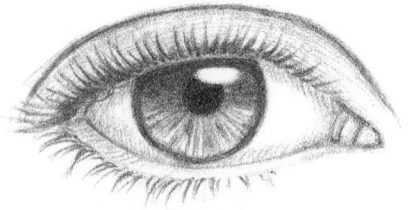

3 Add more color to the iris with radial strokes. Shape the upper and lower eyelids with hatching.

Side View

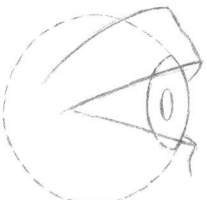

1 Draw a dashed circle, followed by the upper and lower eyelids. Viewed from the side, the iris and pupil are shaped like ellipses, each covered by the eyelid at the top and bottom.

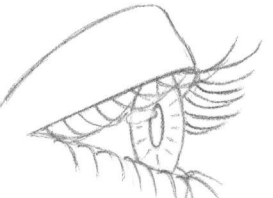

2 When viewed from the side, draw eyelashes from the inner to the outer corner of the eye. The eyelashes are longer above the center of the eye than they are on the sides.

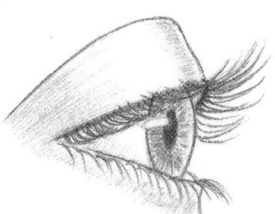

3 When shading the eyelids, work out from the semicircular shape.

Use the guidelines below to practice building out the eyes in front and side views. Don't worry about making it perfect! This is the time to focus on your technique.

Developing Features

After becoming comfortable with drawing the eye itself, start developing the features around the eye, including the eyebrows and the nose. Be sure to space adult eyes about one eye-width apart from each other. And keep in mind that eyes are always glossy—don't forget to add a highlight.

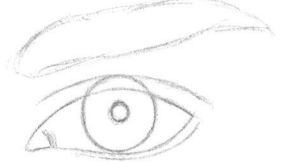 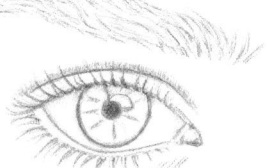 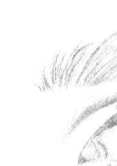

1 Start with a basic outline of the eyes and the eyebrows. Draw the eyes about one eye-width apart from each other.

2 Add a few light strokes to indicate the eyebrows, lashes, and lid and eyeball details.

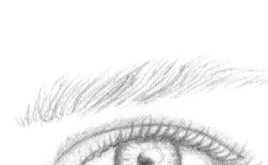 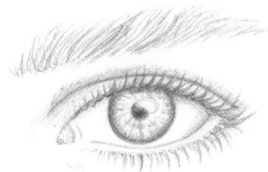 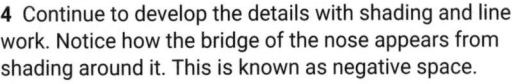

3 Begin to shade the eyes, leaving a white space for the highlight. Eyes should have a glossy feel to them.

4 Continue to develop the details with shading and line work. Notice how the bridge of the nose appears from shading around it. This is known as negative space.

Practice drawing more eyes here, varying their sizes and shapes.

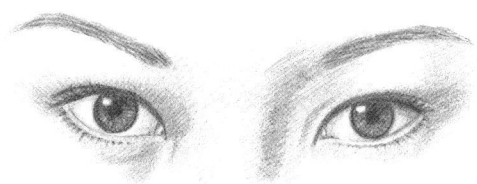

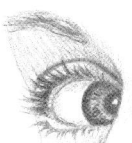

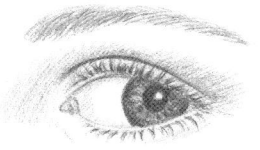

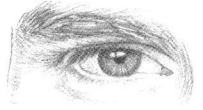

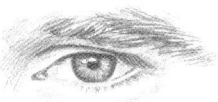

Mouth and Lips

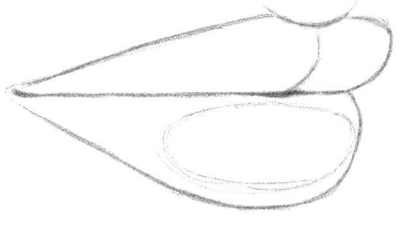

1 First, sketch the basic outline. The top lip slightly protrudes over the bottom lip; the bottom lip is also usually fuller than the top lip.

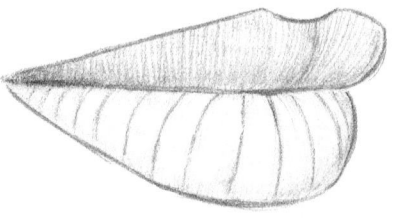

2 Begin shading in the direction of the planes of the lips. The shading on the top lip curves upward, and the shading on the bottom lip curves downward.

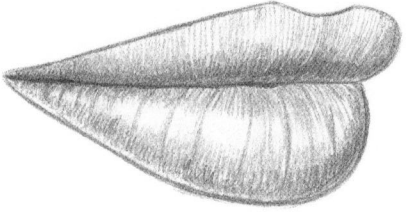

3 Continue shading, making the darkest value at the line where the lips meet. Then lift out some highlights with a kneaded eraser to give them shine and form. Highlights also enhance the lips' fullness, so it's often best to include larger highlights on the fuller bottom lip.

Noses

Noses come in all shapes and sizes. To draw a nose, study the way each plane is lit before adding the dark and light values. The nostrils should be shaded lightly; if they're too dark, they'll draw attention away from the rest of the face.

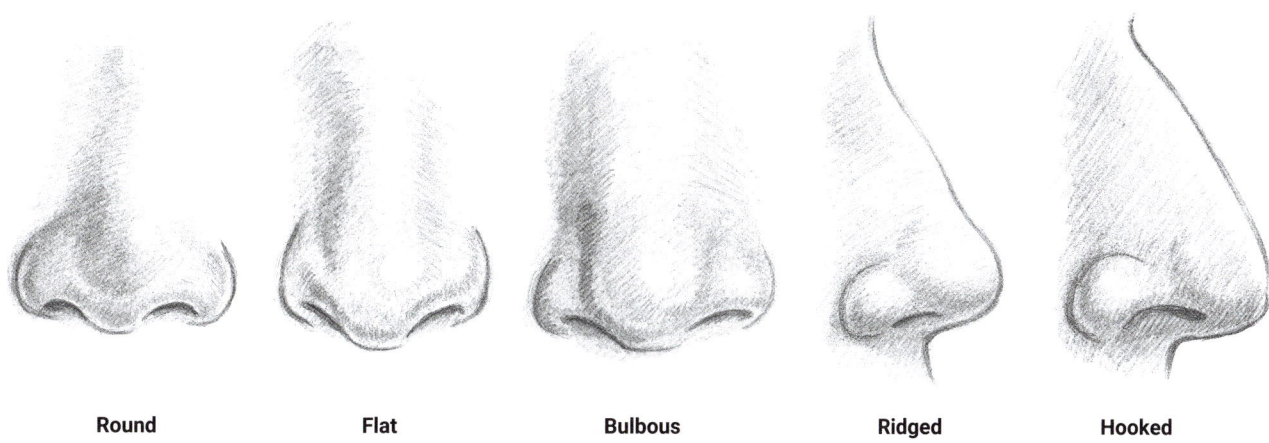

Round   **Flat**   **Bulbous**   **Ridged**   **Hooked**

Capturing the Details

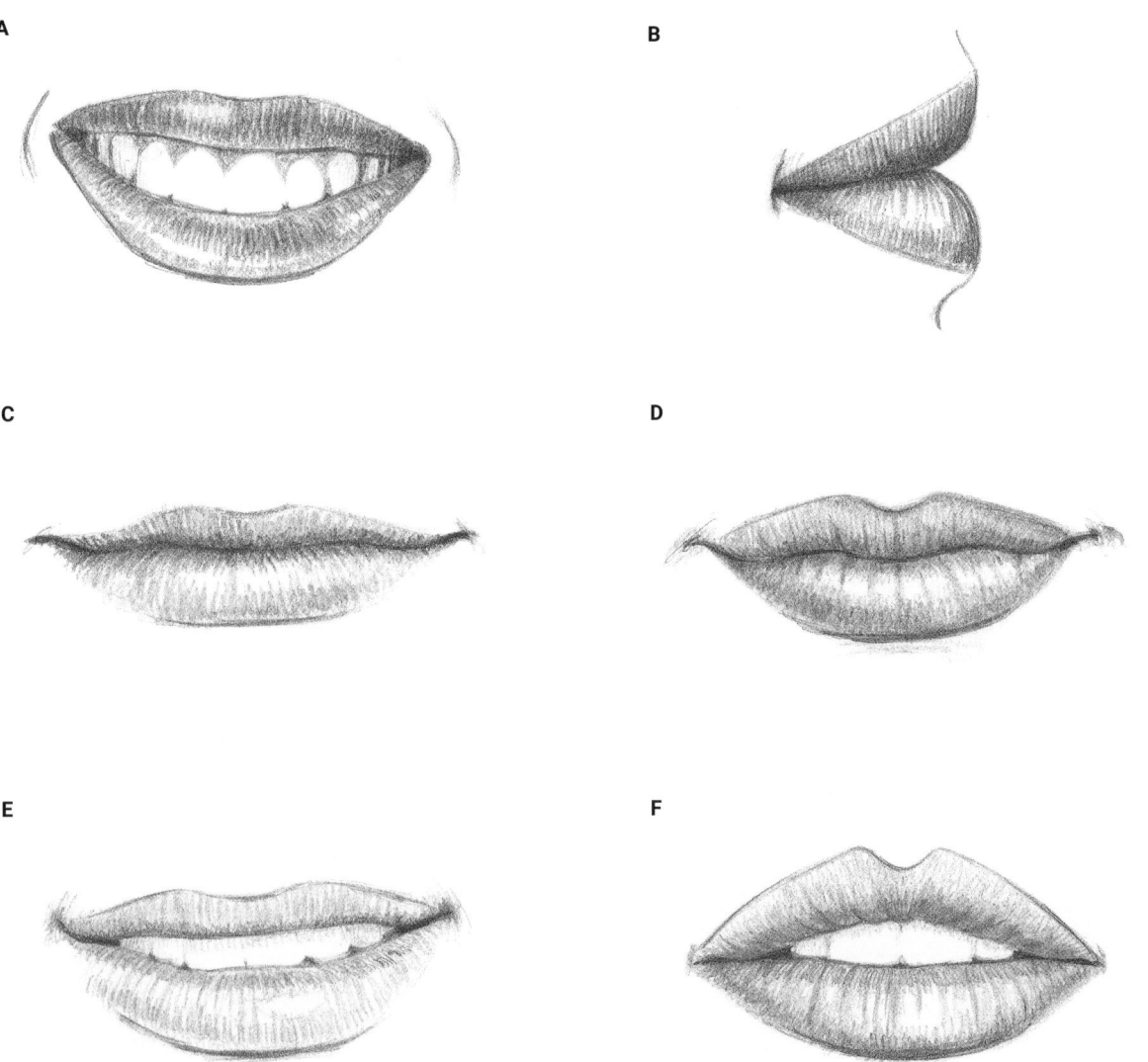

Detailing the Lips Determine how much detail you'd like to add to your renderings of lips. You can add smile lines and dimples (A, B, and D), you can draw clearly defined teeth (A) or parts of the teeth (E and F), or you can draw closed lips (B, C, and D).

Practice drawing a variety of facial features.
See if you are able to combine features successfully
before moving on to the next section.

Combining Features

For beginners, it's easiest to draw the nose and mouth in three steps. First, draw the basic shapes of the upper and lower lips on paper, then gradually add the curved shape using curved lines and hatching. Block out the nose in four vertical planes.

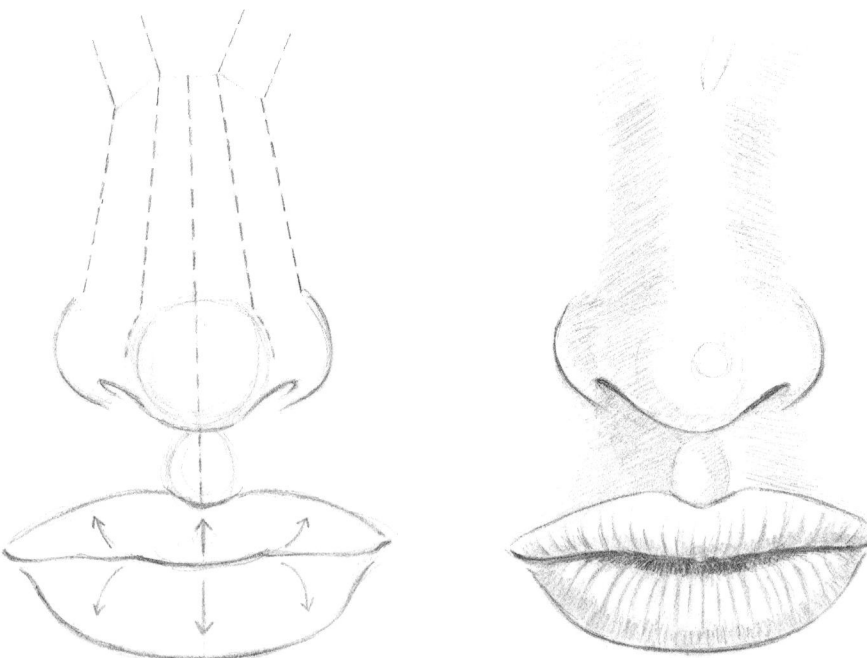

1 Divide the nose into four planes and add a circle on the tip to indicate its roundness. Draw the outline of the lips and add a small circle to connect the base of the nose with the top of the lip. The arrows on the lips indicate the direction of shading.

2 Lightly shade the sides of the nose, nostrils, and the area between the nose and lips. Shade the lips in the direction indicated by the arrows in step 1. Shade the dark area between the top and bottom lips. This helps separate the lips and gives them form.

3 Continue shading to create the forms of the nose and mouth, leaving lighter areas to show reflected light. Use a kneaded eraser to pull out highlights on the top lip and on the tip and bridge of the nose.

Fill in the nose and mouth details using the outline below. Don't forget to add shading and highlights where the light source hits the face.

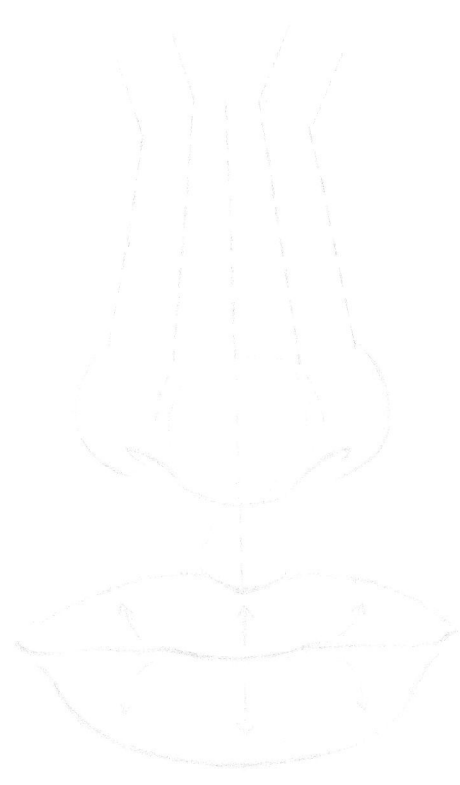

Ears

Ears can be difficult to draw for beginniners. It's tempting to draw the ears perfectly even with the head, but ears generally connect to the head at a slight angle. The width of the ear is usually about one-half of its length.

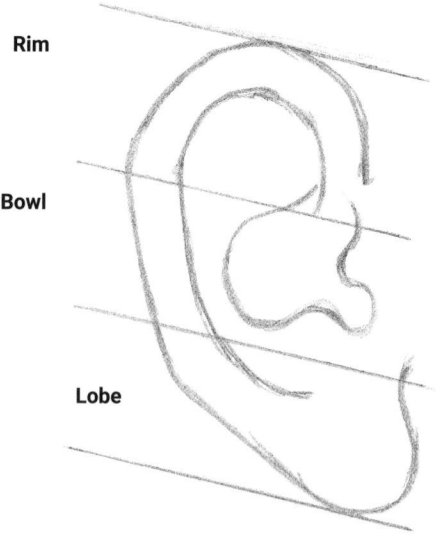

Rim

Bowl

Lobe

1 The ear is shaped like a disk divided into three parts: the rim, the bowl, and the lobe. Start with a basic outline.

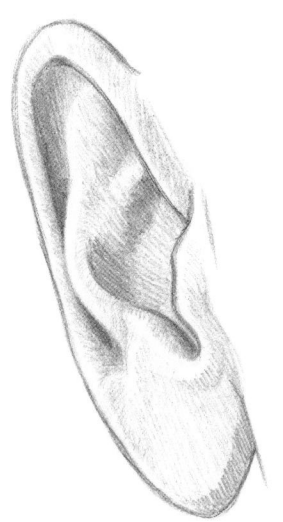

2 Add shading to give the ear form. Apply darker shading inside the folds of the ear to give it dimension.

To develop the ear in profile, block in the general shape in three parts. Shade the darkest areas first, defining the ridges and folds. Then shade the entire ear, leaving highlights in key areas to create the illusion of form.

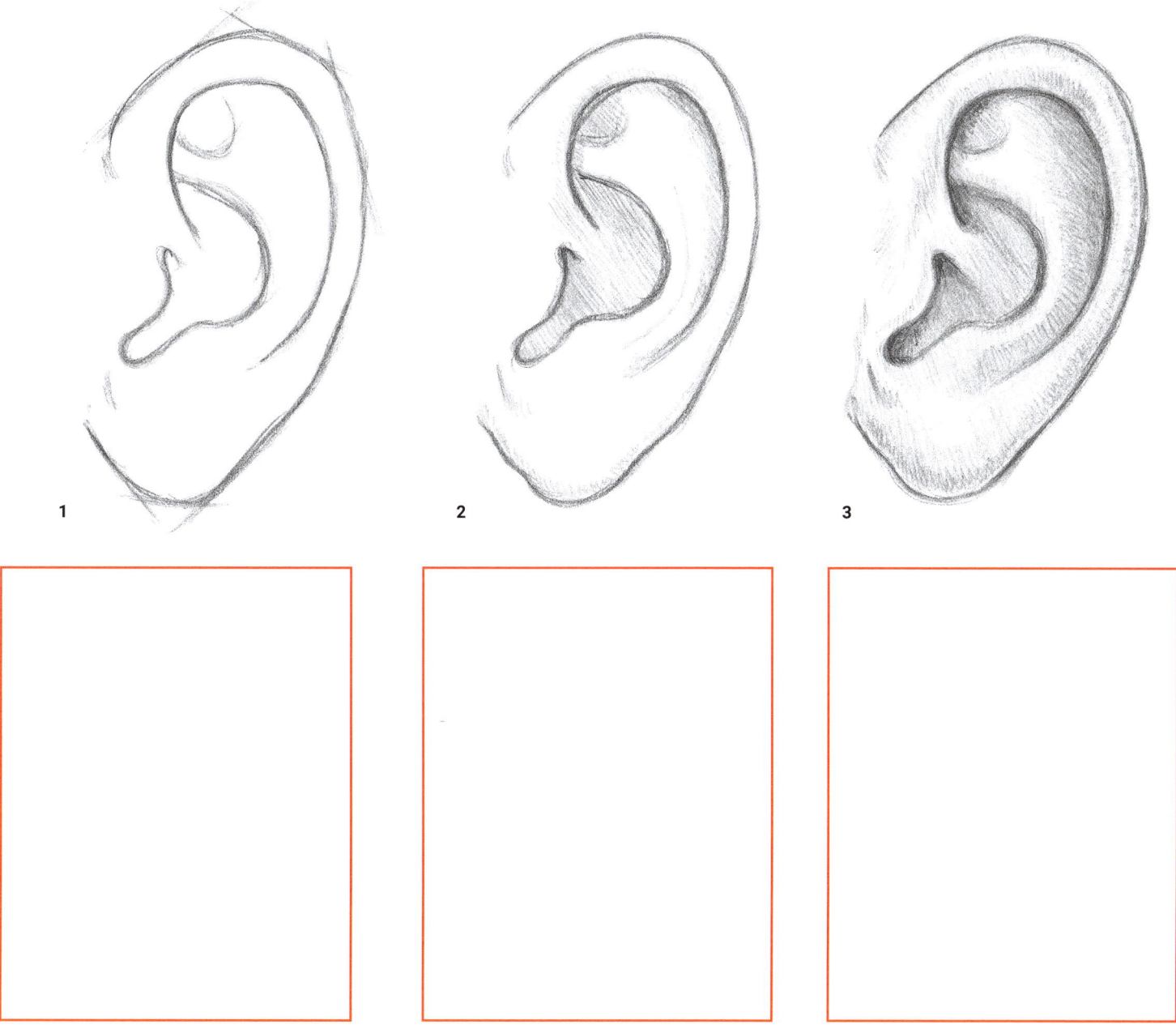

1

2

3

Drawing a Profile

A profile can make for a dramatic drawing. Seeing only one side of the face can bring out a subject's distinctive features, such as a protruding brow, an upturned nose, or a strong chin. Some features appear more prominent in profile, so be careful not to allow any one feature to dominate the drawing.

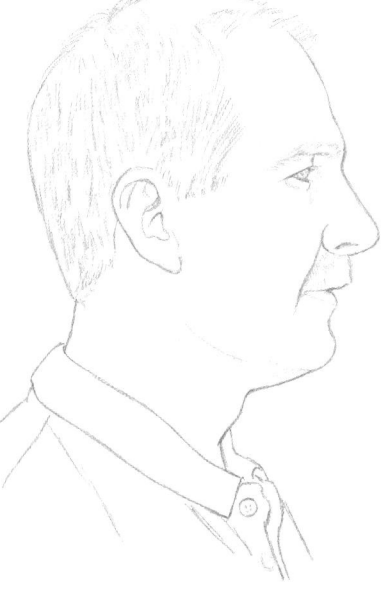

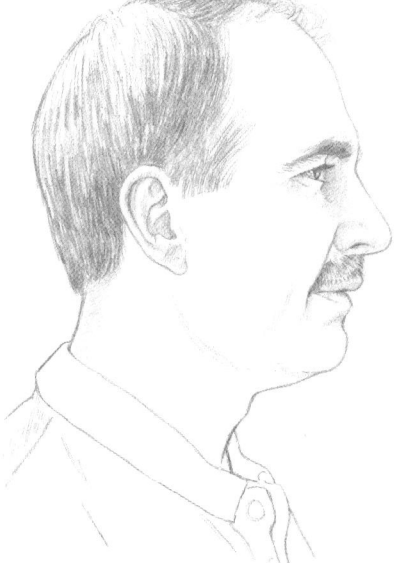

1 In a profile view, the hairline is important because it influences the size and shape of the forehead. This subject has a high forehead, so the hairline starts near the vertical centerline of the cranial mass.

2 Using a 2B pencil, continue building up the forms. Round out the nose and chin; add soft strokes to create the mustache; and suggest the hair using short strokes. Develop the ear, eye, and the eyebrow.

3 Using the 2B, continue to develop the features. Leave white areas in the hair to create the illusion of strands. Add shading to the eye, ear, and nose.

Complete the drawing by adding shading and highlights.

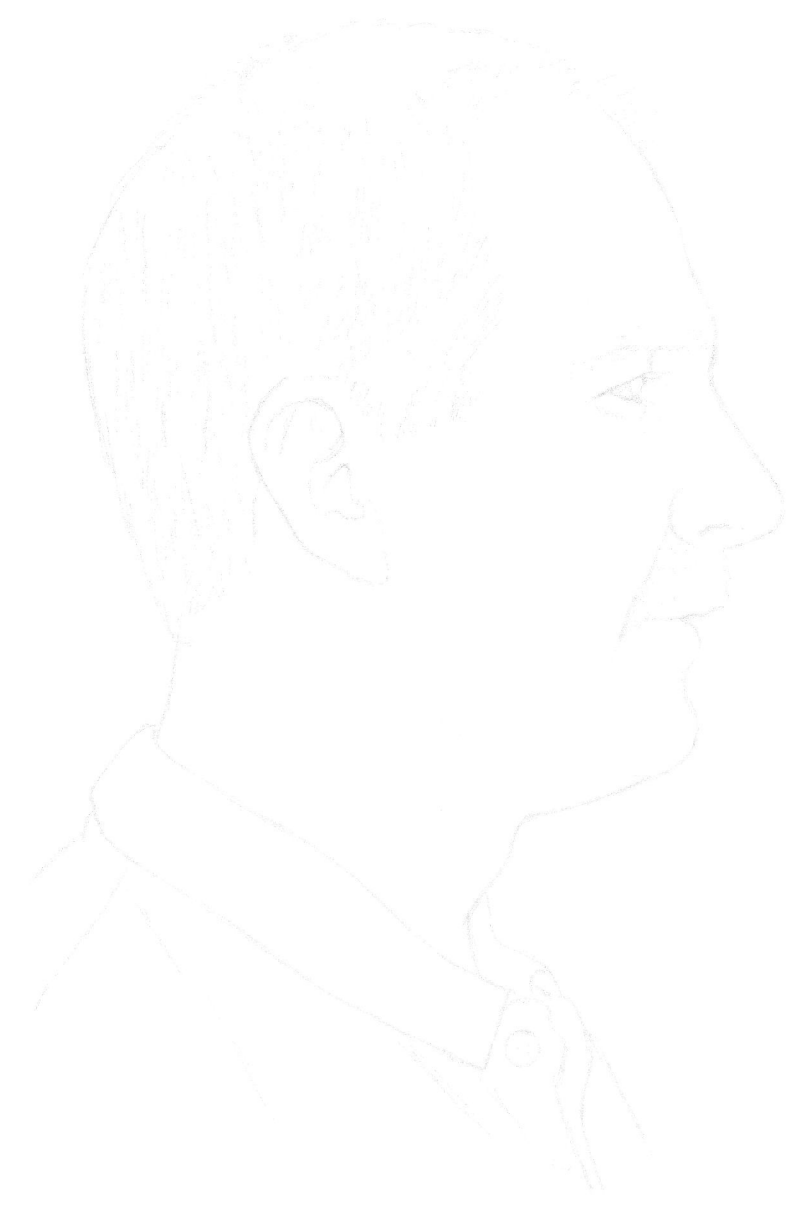

Drawing from a Photograph

If you enjoy drawing portraits, you should move on to drawing people from photographs. Black-and-white photos are best, as they allow you to study the gray tones at your leisure and incorporate them into your drawing.

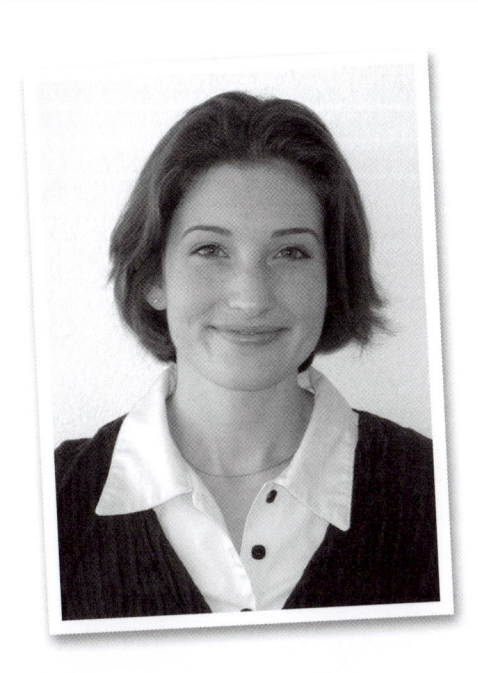

The photo showcases the delicate facial features, skin, and radiant eyes. Pay attention to individual characteristics, such as the slightly crooked mouth, laugh lines, and wide-set eyes. These details are crucial if you want to draw realistic portraits.

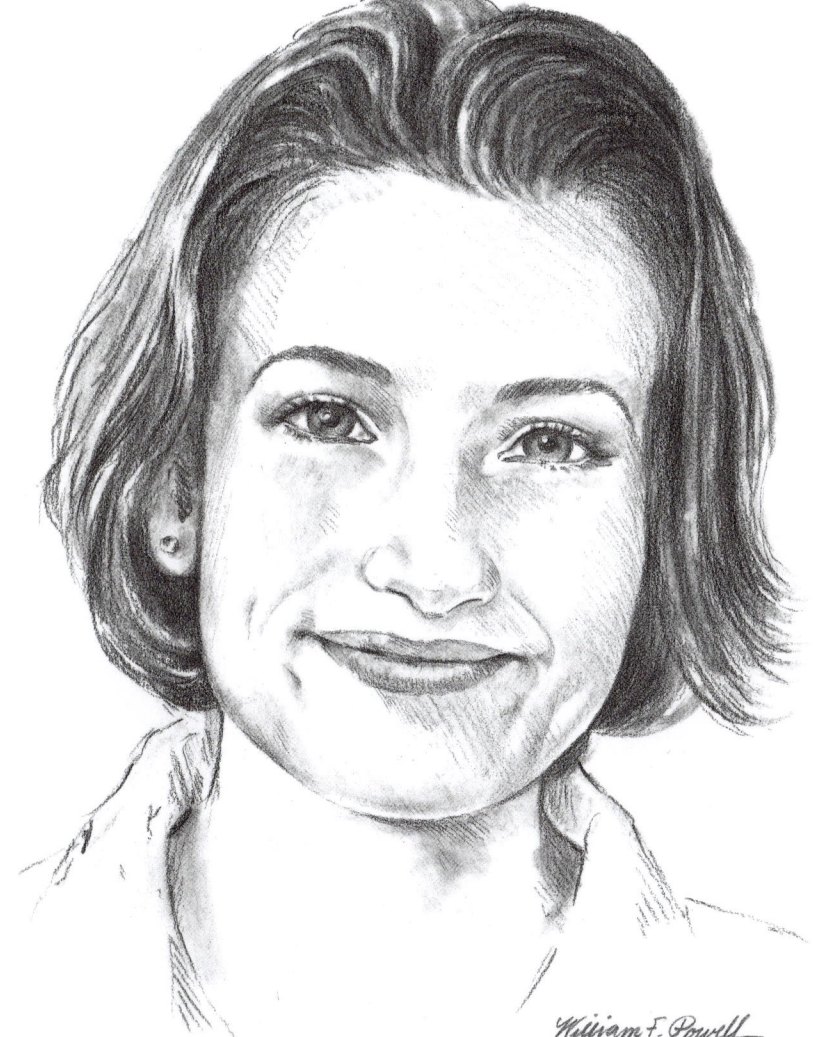

William F. Powell

Draw the iris and pupil, as well as the laugh lines.
It's best to refer to the photo again so you can capture the finer
details of the face. Complete the portrait with shading.

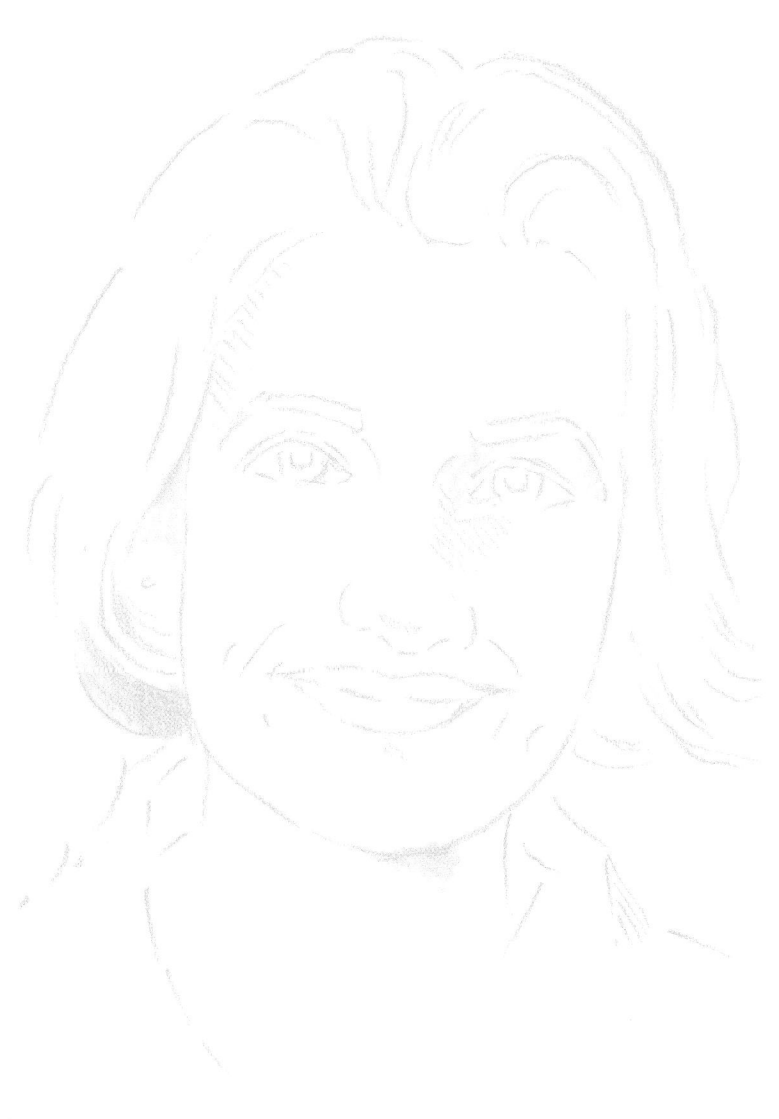

Understanding Lighting

When drawing from a live model, you have an invaluable advantage: You can position the model in the light you like. When working outdoors, the model can change position until you're satisfied. In the studio, you adjust the lighting until everything is just right.

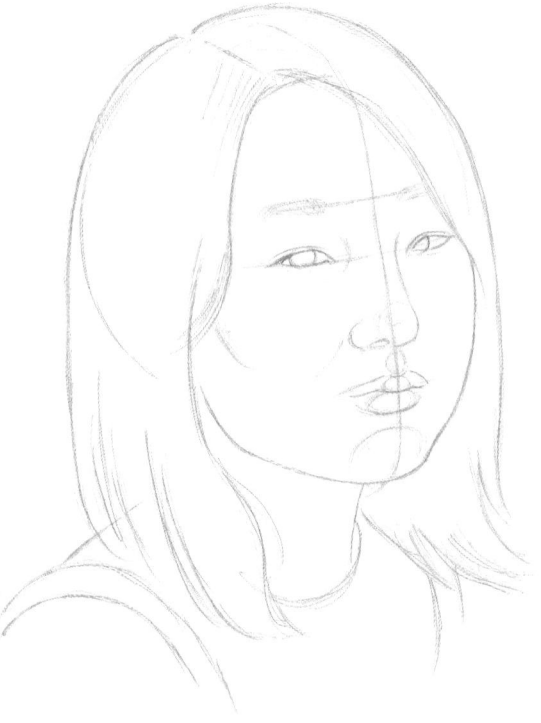

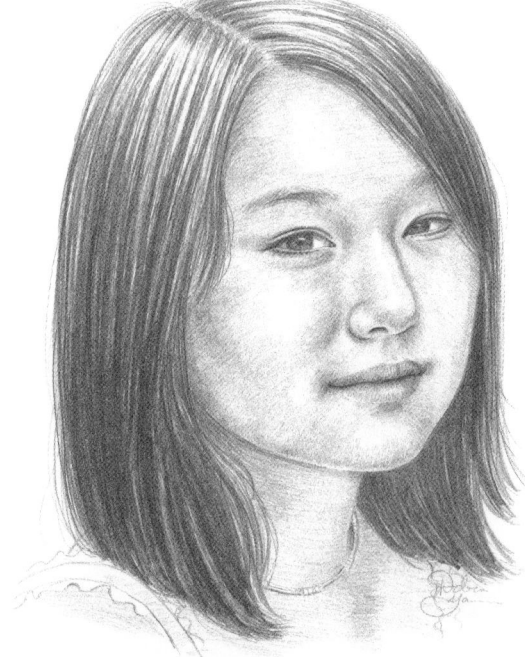

1 Block out the face in a three-quarter view, using broad shapes and light sketch lines. Note that one nostril is visible, and the mouth appears shorter on the left than on the right.

2 Using a 3B pencil, darken the hair. Then use a variety of shading techniques to add depth and form to the face. Use a kneaded eraser to lift out highlights or to soften pencil strokes.

Draw the hair with a 2H pencil, and leave plenty of white space for the highlights. Use light horizontal strokes to suggest the shape of the neck. Then add shading as needed.

Capturing a Likeness

Once you've practiced drawing the individual features, you're ready to combine them in a full portrait. Use your understanding of proportion to block in the head and place the features. Study your subject carefully so you can capture their unique attributes in your drawing.

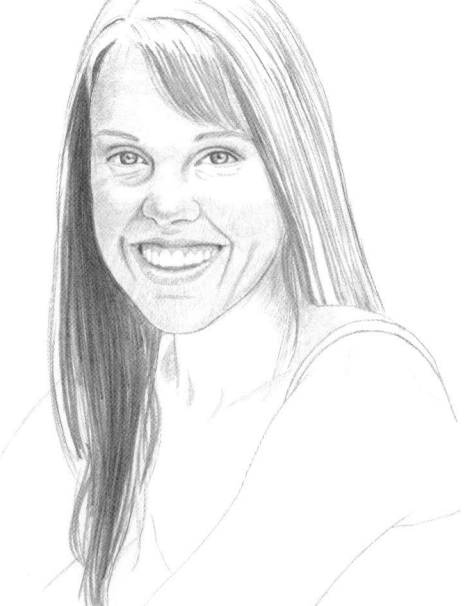

1 Using an HB pencil, sketch the general outline of the subject's face. Then place the facial guidelines before blocking in the eyes, nose, and mouth. Block in the shape of the hair, including the bangs.

2 Switching to a 2B pencil, indicate the roundness of the facial features, focusing on the things that make this individual unique, such as the turned-up nose and wide smile.

3 Begin shading, following the form of the face. Use a 2B pencil and softly blend to create the smoothness of the skin. Next, create the teeth, lightly indicating the separations with incomplete lines. Finally, lay in more dark streaks of hair.

Fill in the details of this portrait using the outline below.

Including a Background

An effective background will draw the viewer's eye to your subject and play a role in setting a mood. A background should complement a drawing without detracting from the subject. A light, neutral setting will enhance a subject with dark hair or skin, while a dark background will set off a subject with light hair or skin.

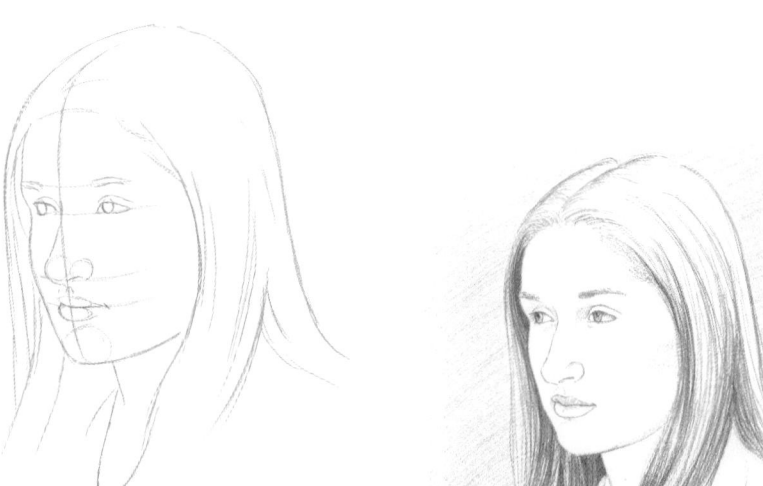

1 With an HB pencil, sketch the basic head shape and the guidelines, and then block in the position of the eyes, brows, nose, mouth, neck, and hair.

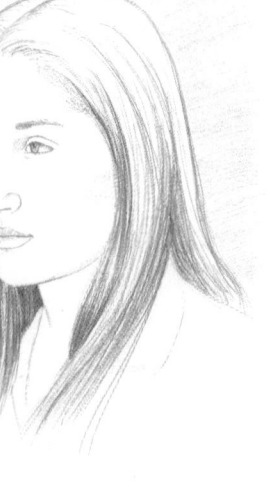

2 Using a 2B pencil, develop facial features and shade the irises. Use a 3B pencil to build up the dark values of the hair, curving the strokes around the face. Add light shading to the background using diagonal hatching strokes.

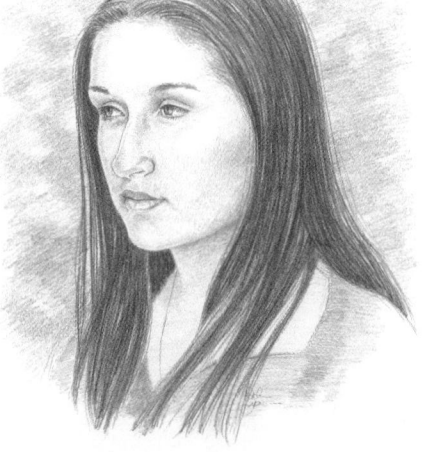

3 Finish shading the face, neck, and shirt with a 2B pencil, and add more dark streaks to the hair. Apply another layer of strokes to the background, carefully working around the hair. Use a kneaded eraser to smooth out the transitions.

Complete this portrait using the outline below. Add shading to the background and then use a blending stump to smooth it out.

Depicting Age

As we age, our skin's elasticity decreases: Wrinkles appear, the nose and ears droop slightly, and lips become thinner. Many older people wear glasses. Consider these traits when drawing a person of advanced age.

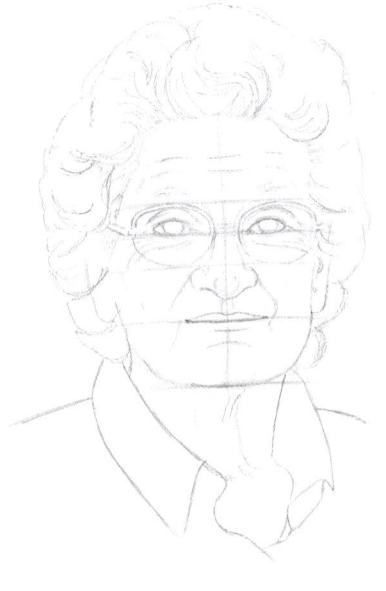

1 Block in the face, glasses, and delicate lines around the eyes. Add the wrinkles on the forehead.

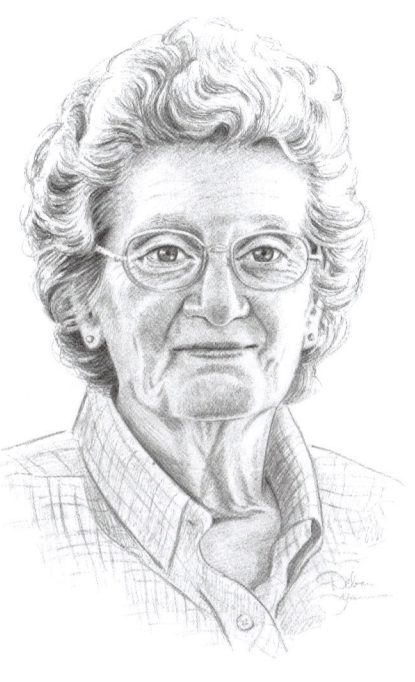

2 Deepen the wrinkles around the eyes so they don't blend into the surface of the face. Continue to add shading to refine the details.

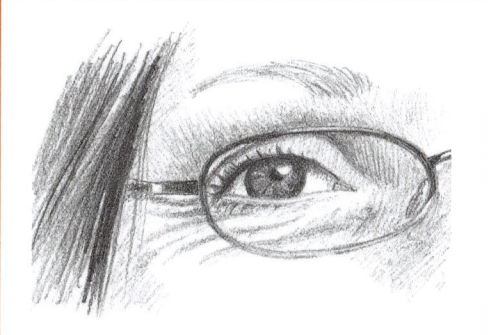

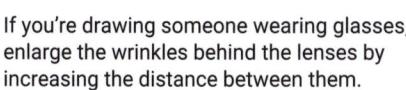

If you're drawing someone wearing glasses, enlarge the wrinkles behind the lenses by increasing the distance between them.

Use a 2B pencil to fill in the wrinkles around the eyes, neck, and face.
Pay attention to the hatching around the mouth and nose to create
the impression of soft skin. Practice drawing faces of all ages.

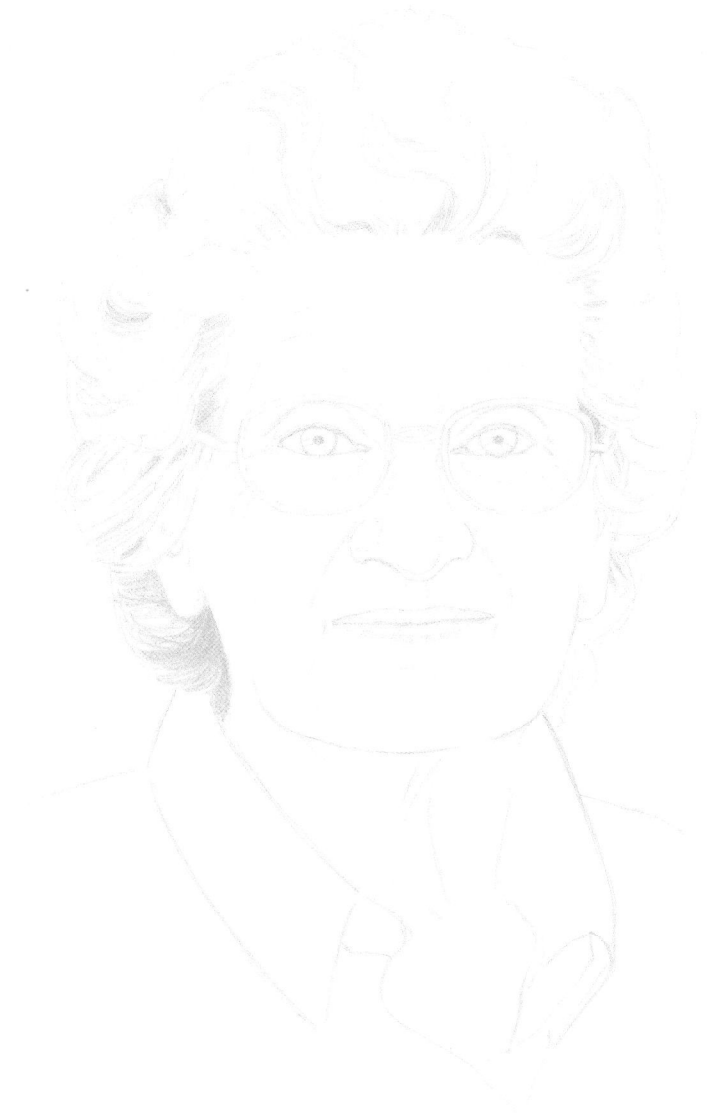

Children's Faces

Children's proportions are different than those of adults: Young children have rounder faces with larger eyes that are spaced farther apart. Their features also are positioned a little lower on the face. As a child ages, the shape of the face elongates, altering the proportions.

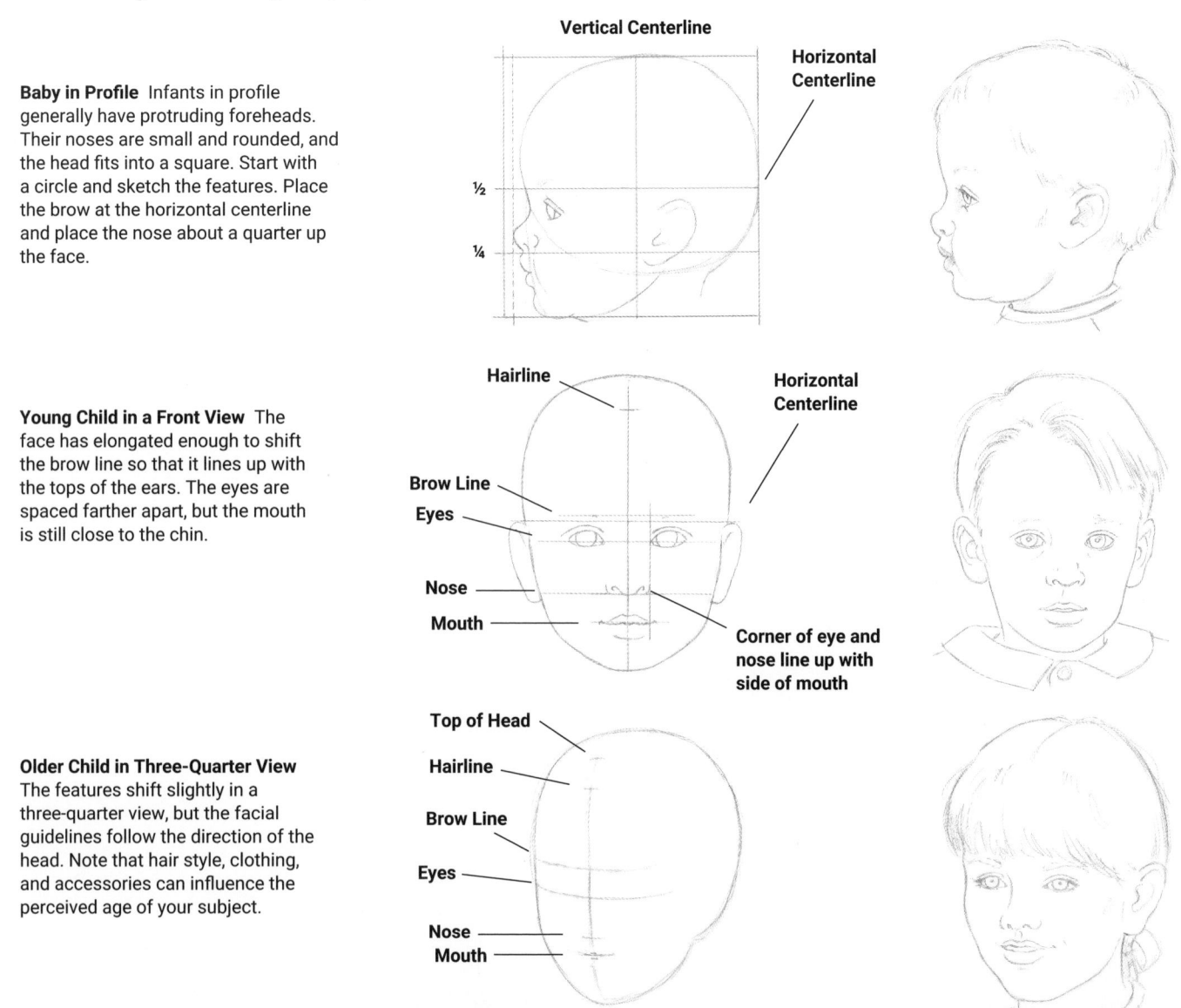

Baby in Profile Infants in profile generally have protruding foreheads. Their noses are small and rounded, and the head fits into a square. Start with a circle and sketch the features. Place the brow at the horizontal centerline and place the nose about a quarter up the face.

Vertical Centerline

Horizontal Centerline

½

¼

Young Child in a Front View The face has elongated enough to shift the brow line so that it lines up with the tops of the ears. The eyes are spaced farther apart, but the mouth is still close to the chin.

Hairline

Horizontal Centerline

Brow Line

Eyes

Nose

Mouth

Corner of eye and nose line up with side of mouth

Older Child in Three-Quarter View The features shift slightly in a three-quarter view, but the facial guidelines follow the direction of the head. Note that hair style, clothing, and accessories can influence the perceived age of your subject.

Top of Head

Hairline

Brow Line

Eyes

Nose

Mouth

Practice drawing a child's facial features using the outline below.

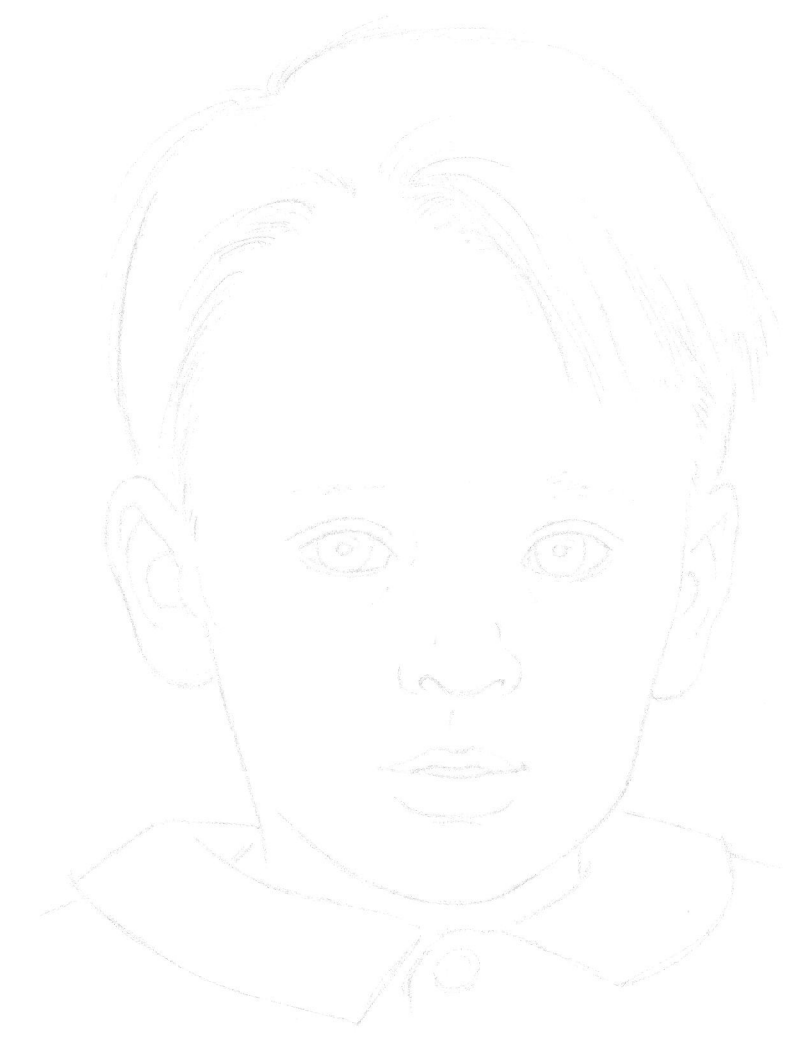

Changing Over Time

The placement of the features in children changes as the face becomes longer and thinner with age. Use horizontal guidelines to divide the area from the horizontal centerline to the chin into equal sections; these lines can be used to determine where to the place the features.

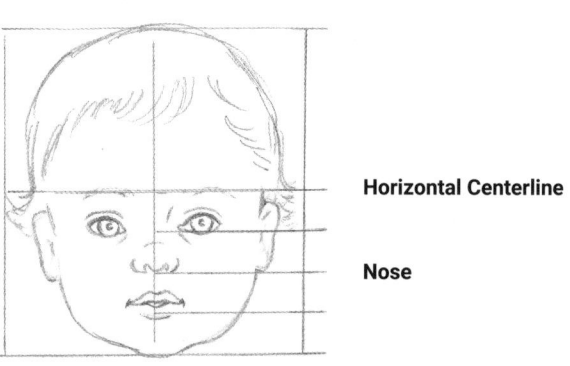

Vertical Centerline

Horizontal Centerline

Nose

Drawing an Infant A baby's head is square shaped. They have larger foreheads, and their eyebrows fall on the horizontal centerline. Their eyes are large in relation to the other features.

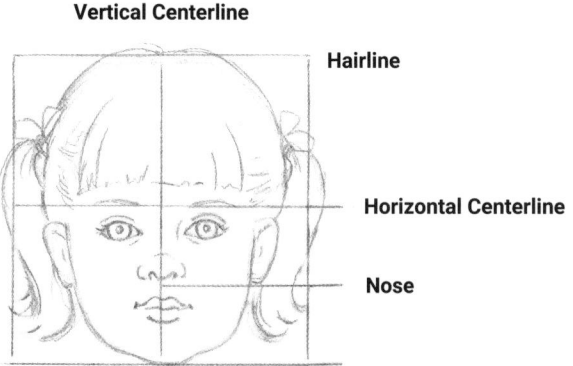

Vertical Centerline

Hairline

Horizontal Centerline

Nose

Drawing a Toddler As a toddler, the forehead shortens, the chin elongates, and the bottoms of the eyebrows meet the horizontal centerline. The eyes are also closer together.

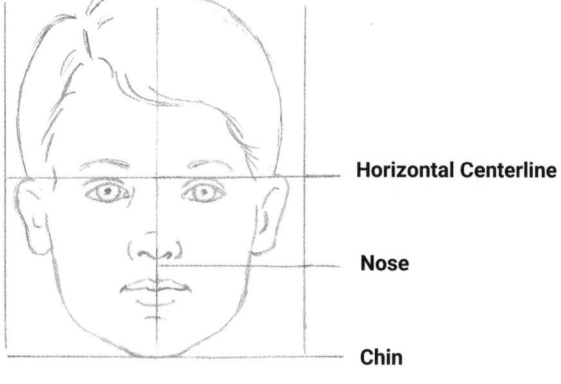

Horizontal Centerline

Nose

Chin

Drawing a Child As young child, the face lengthens and the eyebrows move above the horizontal centerline. The ears line up with the bottom of the nose.

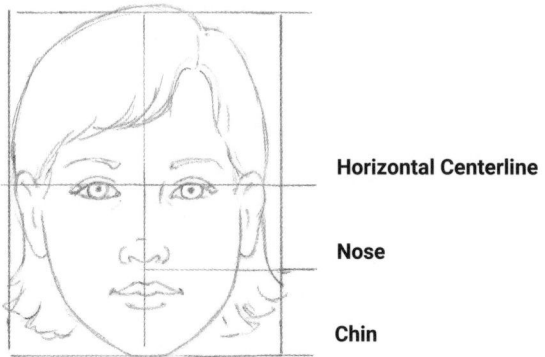

Horizontal Centerline

Nose

Chin

Drawing a Teenager A teenager's face is longer and oval shaped. The eyes are nearly at the horizontal centerline, and the tops of the ears are about even with the eyebrows.

Practice placing features using the guidelines below.

Children's Features

Children are fascinating drawing subjects, but they can be a challenge to draw accurately. It's important to get the right proportions for the particular age and to correctly render their features.

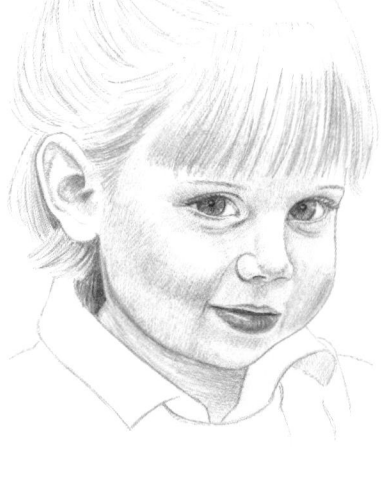

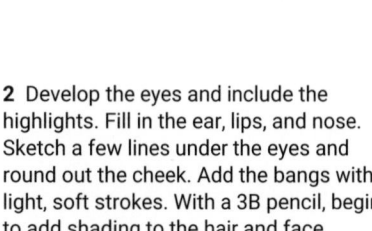

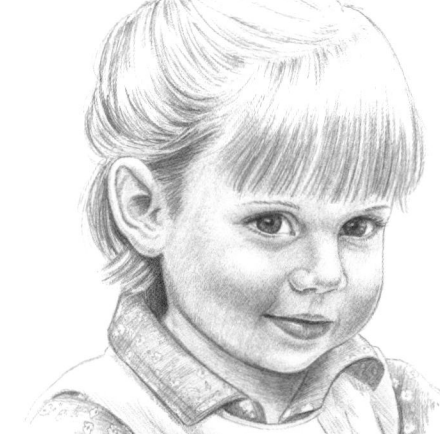

1 With a sharpened 2B pencil, sketch the basic shape of the face and the guidelines. Block in the eyes and place the other features. Add some wispy hair to frame the face, and outline the collar of the outfit.

2 Develop the eyes and include the highlights. Fill in the ear, lips, and nose. Sketch a few lines under the eyes and round out the cheek. Add the bangs with light, soft strokes. With a 3B pencil, begin to add shading to the hair and face.

3 Using a 2B pencil, shade the ear and lips, and define the lines around the eyes and mouth. Shade the neck, eyebrows, and around the cheeks. Use long strokes to build up the bangs. Use a 3B pencil to add texture to the outfit. Lift out highlights with a kneaded eraser.

Practice your shading techniques using the outline below.

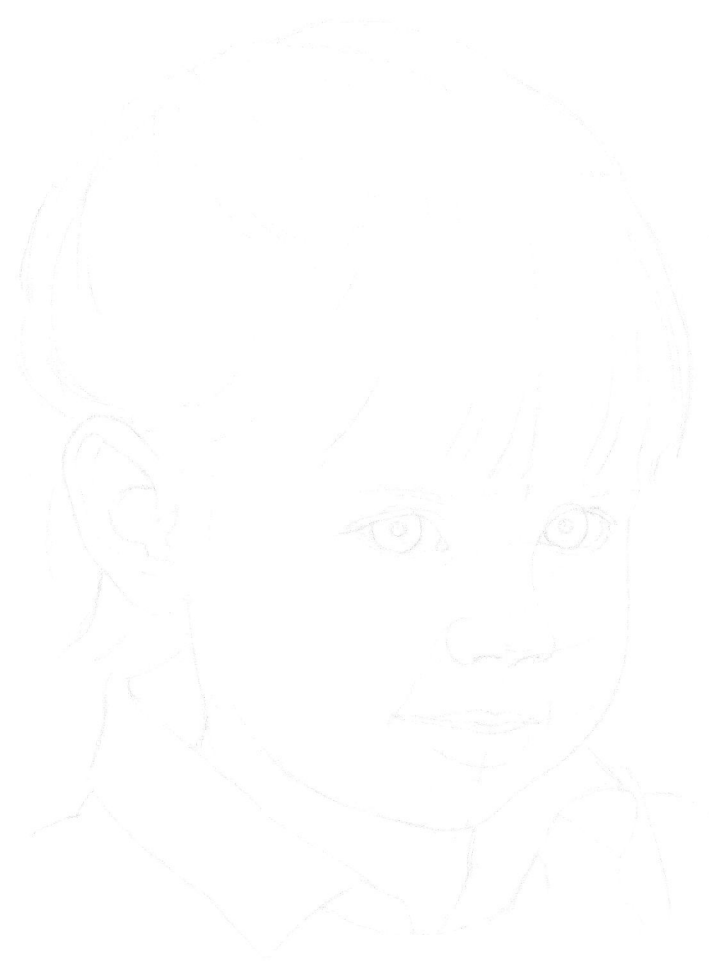

Drawing a Baby

Drawing babies can be tricky because it's easy to unintentionally make them look older than they are. The face gets longer in proportion to the cranium with age, so the younger the child, the lower the eyes are on the face (and thus, the larger the forehead). In addition, babies' eyes are disproportionately large in comparison to the rest of their bodies, so make sure to draw them this way.

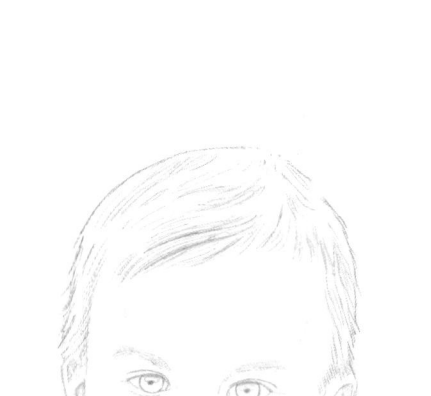

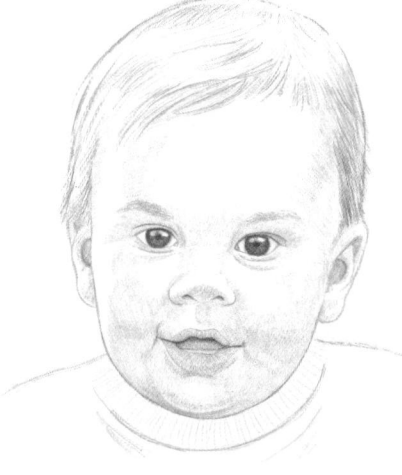

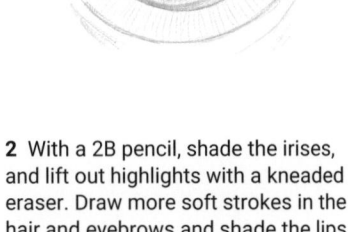

1 Using an HB pencil, block in the head and face. Place the features, and draw the hair using a B pencil. Draw a curved line under the chin to suggest a chubby face. Indicate the shoulders, but omit the neck. Add pupils and highlights to the eyes with a B pencil.

2 With a 2B pencil, shade the irises, and lift out highlights with a kneaded eraser. Draw more soft strokes in the hair and eyebrows and shade the lips and face.

3 Continue to add shading, and use a kneaded eraser to pull out highlights. Draw some light eyelashes. Create darker values in the hair and eyebrows, and darken the outline of the face. Use a blending stump to softly blend transitions in your shading.

Select an infant model of your choosing, whether it's someone you know or from a photo reference. Sketch the portrait in the space provided.

Basic Anatomy

For many years, leaders in fields as diverse as medicine, science, sports, and art have marveled at the form and function of the human body. In truth, the information an artist needs to know about the body and its basic anatomy has barely changed since the time of Leonardo da Vinci. Artistic anatomy explores what creates and influences that form. Having a basic understanding of anatomy can help make your drawings even more realistic and proportional.

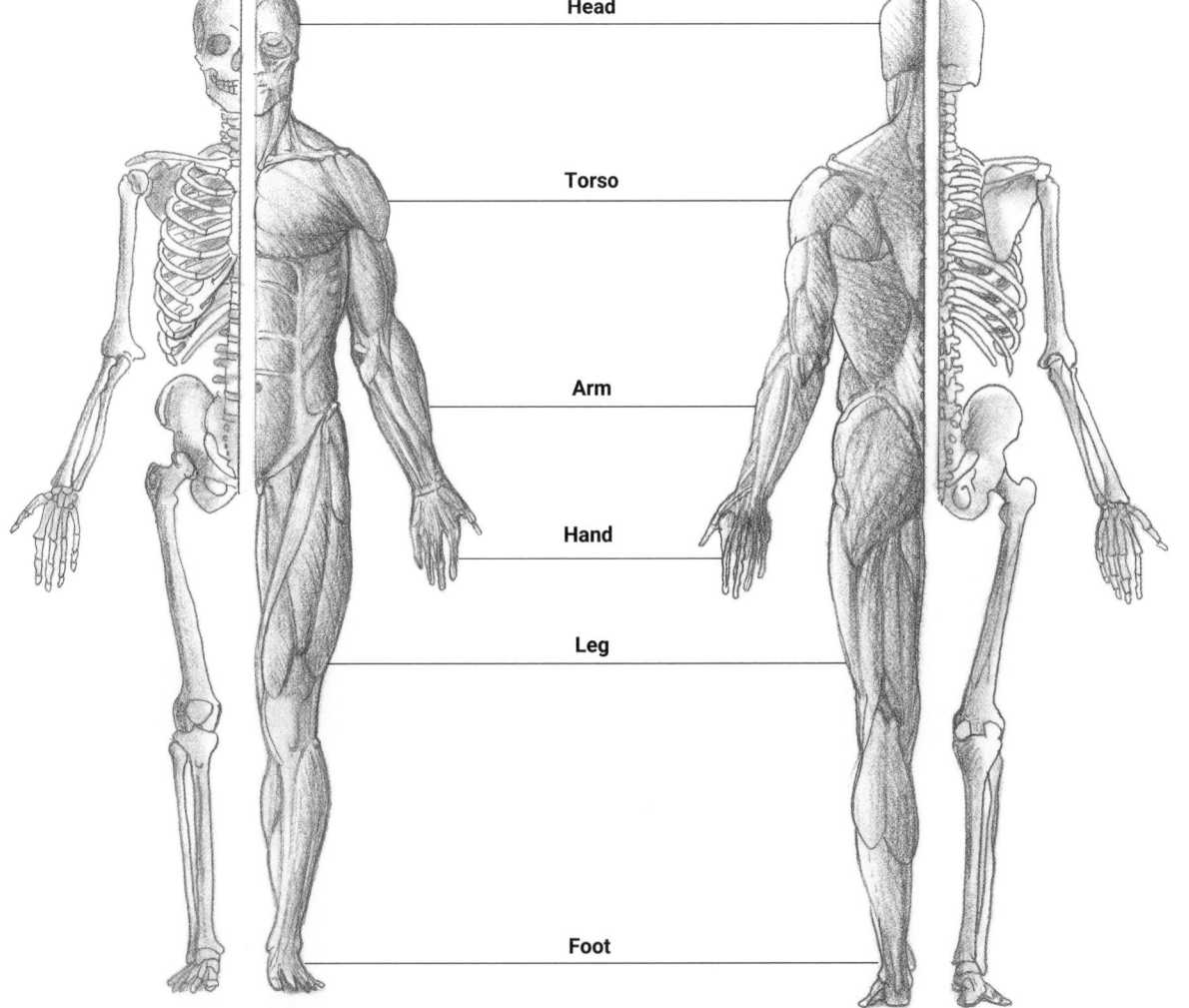

Head

Torso

Arm

Hand

Leg

Foot

These illustrations show many of the bones and muscles you'll want to study
if you are to master drawing the human form.

Front View

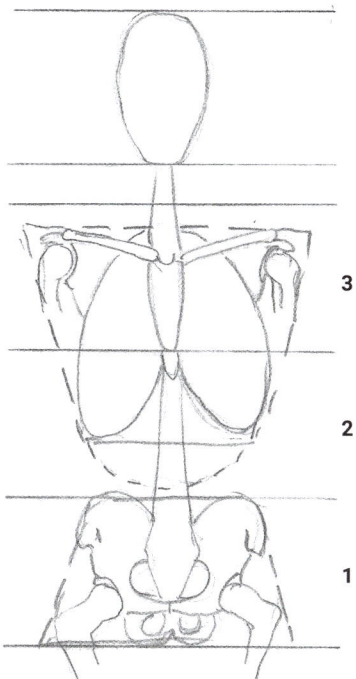

3

2

1

Sketching with simple lines and basic shapes is a good way to establish the base of a figure drawing.

Back View

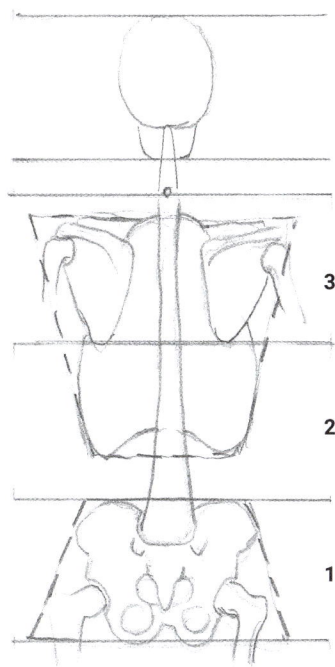

3

2

1

Trapezoids represent the overall bone structure of the torso from both front and rear views. Here you can see the same three-part division.

Side View

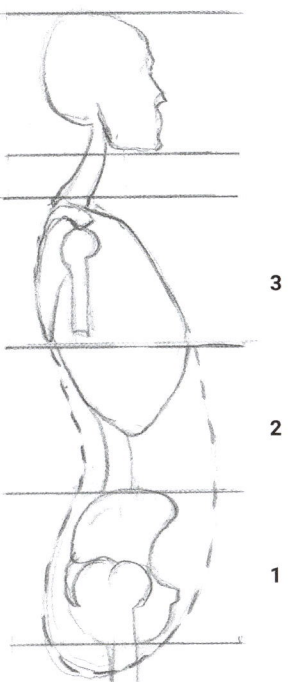

3

2

1

The simplified torso from the side view has a bean-shaped appearance, but the same proportional divisions of the torso apply.

Adult Body Proportions

The proportional measurements of the human body vary slightly for every person; however, studying average human proportions is helpful when learning to draw. The human form is measured in "heads": The vertical distance from the top of the head to the chin. If one part of the body appears too large or too small, you can correct the problem by adjusting it according to its size in heads.

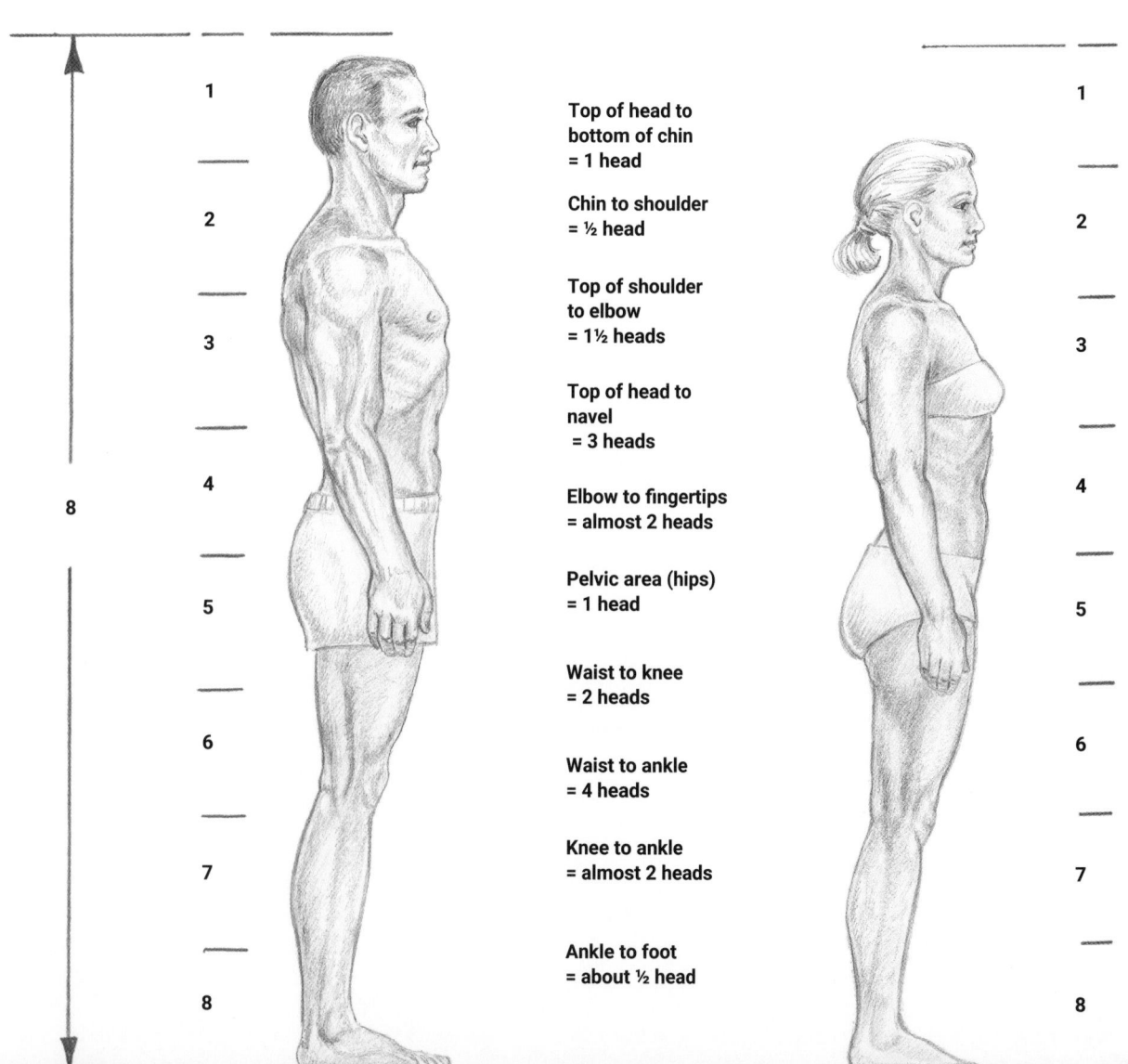

Top of head to bottom of chin = 1 head

Chin to shoulder = ½ head

Top of shoulder to elbow = 1½ heads

Top of head to navel = 3 heads

Elbow to fingertips = almost 2 heads

Pelvic area (hips) = 1 head

Waist to knee = 2 heads

Waist to ankle = 4 heads

Knee to ankle = almost 2 heads

Ankle to foot = about ½ head

Use the guide below to practice placing the figure in correct proportion.
Remember: The body is measured in heads.

1

2

3

4

8

5

6

7

8

1

2

3

4

5

6

7

8

Developing Form

Try drawing these three views as often as you like until you're familiar with the basic shape of the human body from the front, back, and side. Creating a figure with a few lines and simple shapes is another way to approach this kind of drawing.

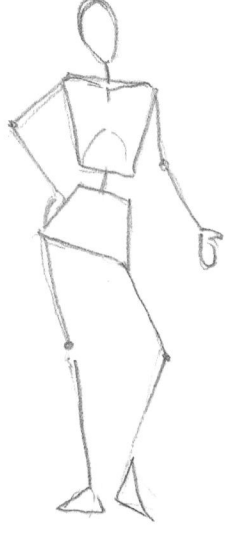

Front View

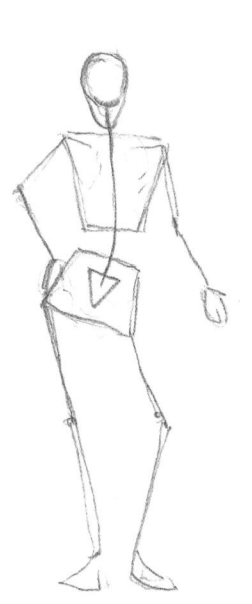

Back View

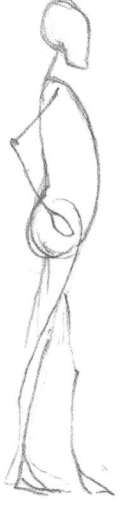

Side View

Pay attention to the centerline: a vertical guideline that divides the body in half. Adjust the centerline to move with the natural movement of the body. This ensures correct proportion.

The human body can be reduced to a few basic shapes.
Once you're comfortable with drawing the body as line art,
build out those shapes into three-dimensional forms.

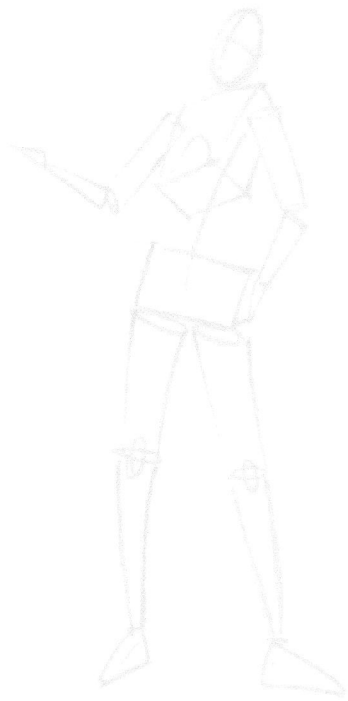

Child Body Proportions

Children make great drawing subjects. If you're observing your own model, measure how many heads make up the height of the subject's body. Begin the drawing by lightly sketching a stick figure. Use simple shapes, such as circles, ovals, and rectangles to block in the body. Continue to develop them into a completed form, and add the outline of the clothing.

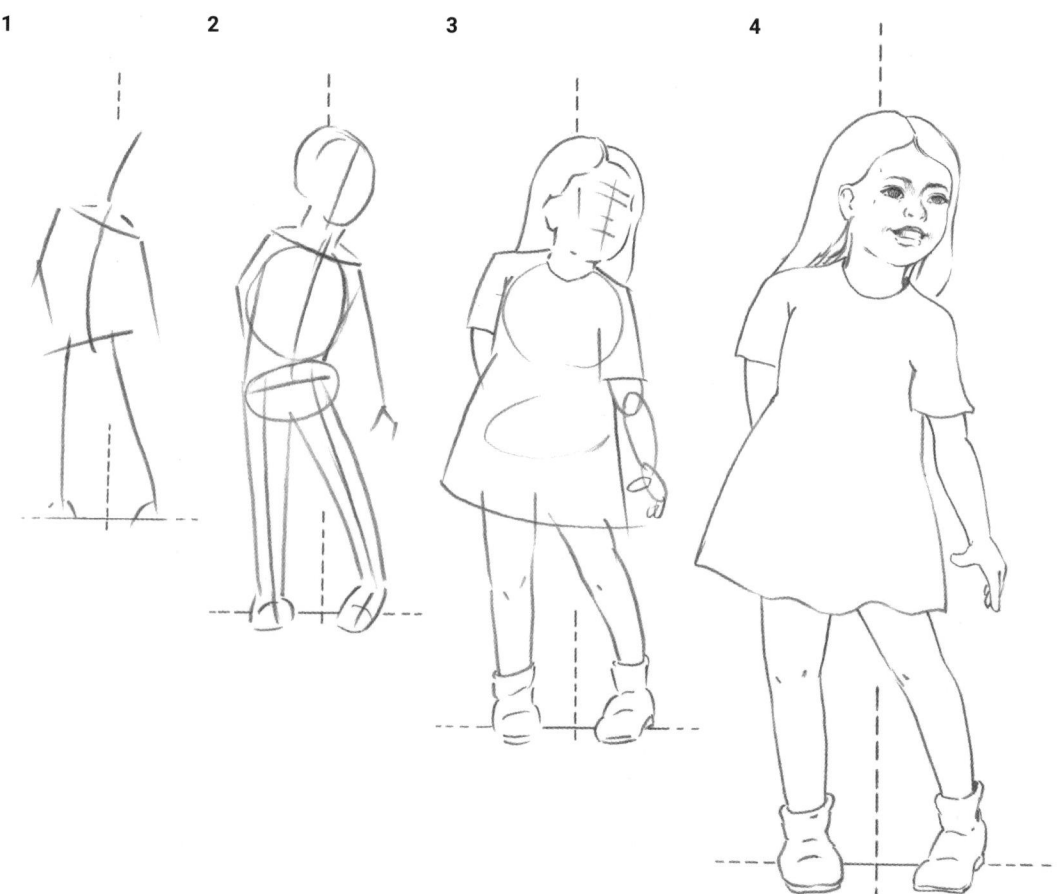

1   2   3   4

Practice drawing this child's proportions using the outlines below.

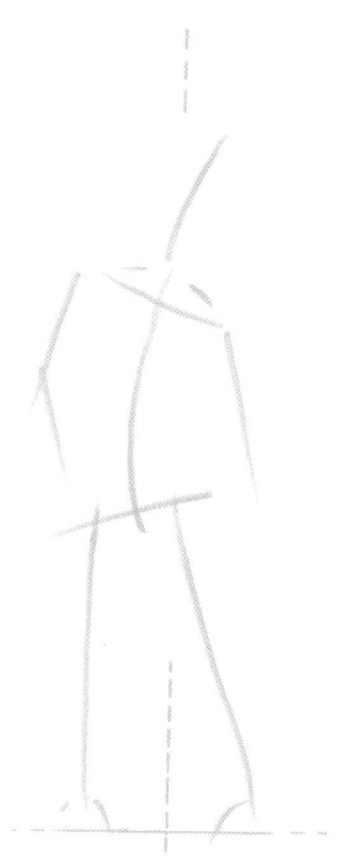

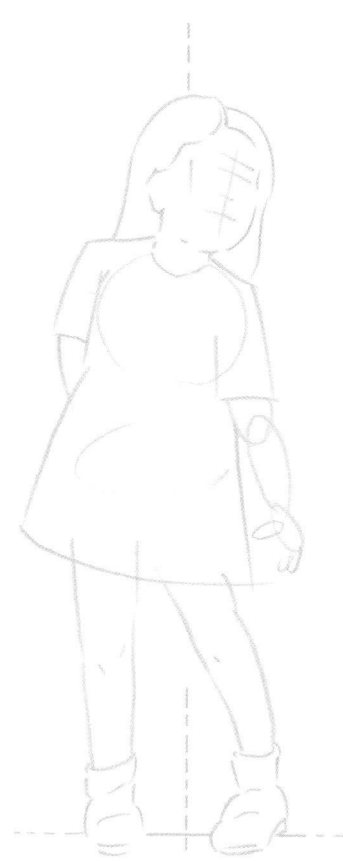

Drawing Hands

Hands are highly expressive body parts, which can make them an artistic challenge. To familiarize yourself with the proportions of a hand, first draw three curved lines that are all the same distance apart. The fingertips all end on the outer line, the second joints on the second line, and the knuckles begin on the third line. The first finger joint is approximately halfway between the first and second lines, and the palm is the same length as the middle finger.

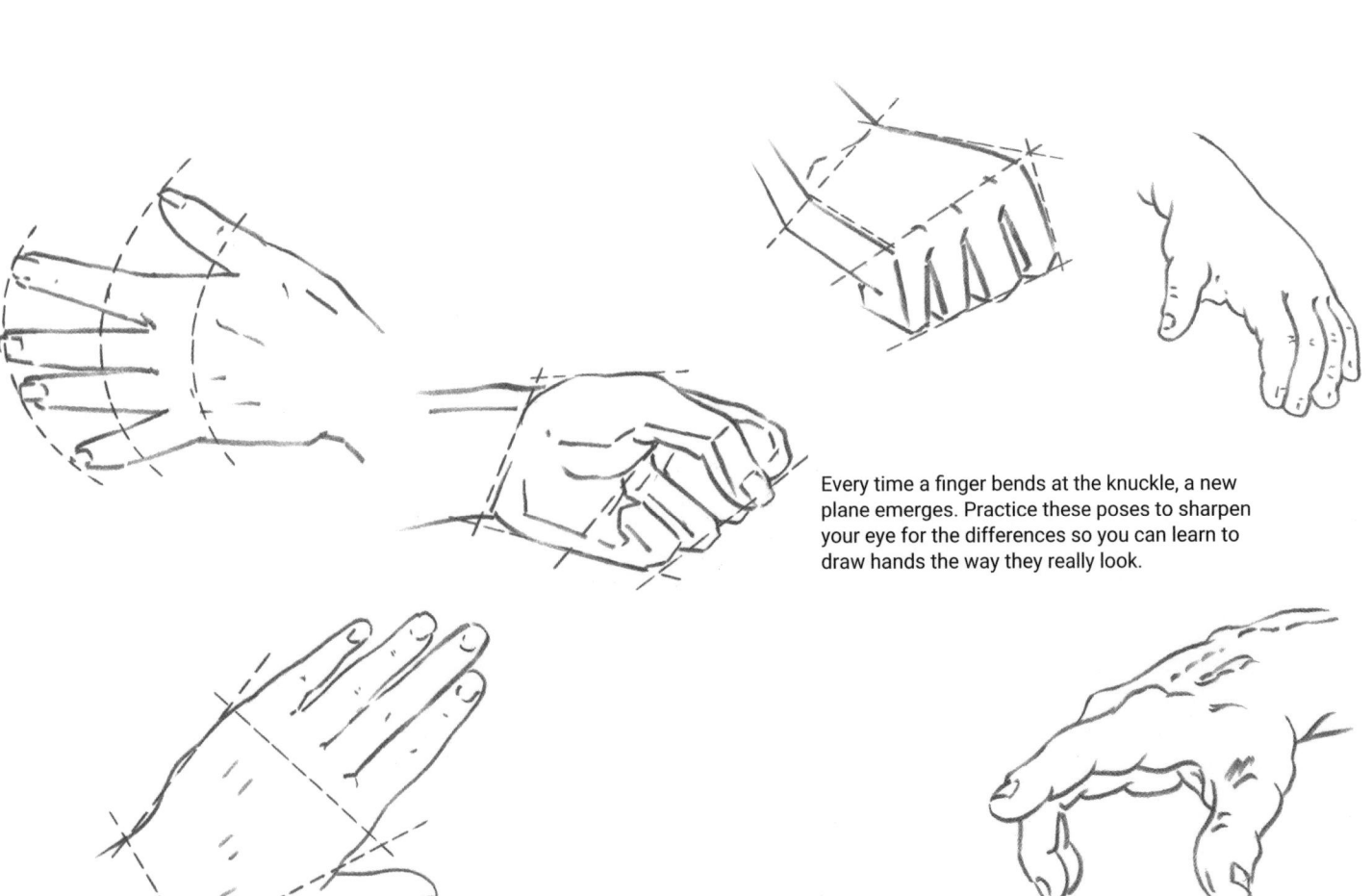

Every time a finger bends at the knuckle, a new plane emerges. Practice these poses to sharpen your eye for the differences so you can learn to draw hands the way they really look.

Your own hands are the best model. Draw your hand, or someone else's, moving it into different positions. Observe the light and shadows and draw what you see.

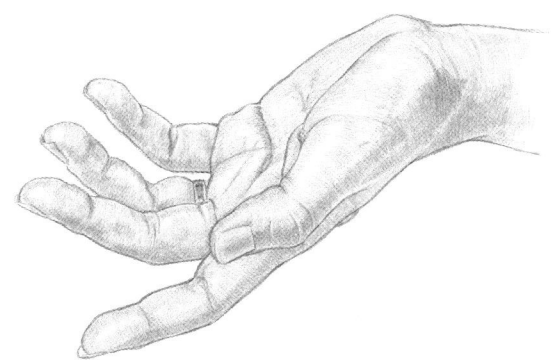

Hand Size

When sizing a hand to a figure, remember that a hand is about the same length as the face, from chin to hairline. Try not to be discouraged if your first few drawings aren't lifelike; hands definitely take a lot of practice!

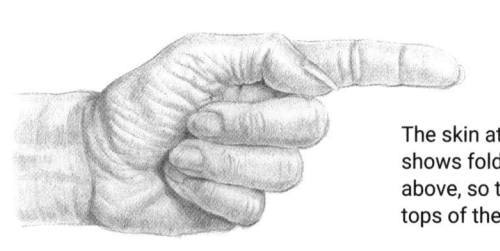

The skin at the base of the thumb shows folds. This hand is lit from above, so the highlights are on the tops of the fingers.

This hand holds a paintbrush, but the same pose could hold a pen or pencil. The light source from the right highlights the fingers.

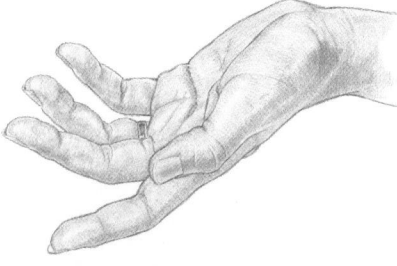

An open palm shows a hand at rest or reaching for something. The light source is from above, so the highlights are on the tops of the fingers and palm.

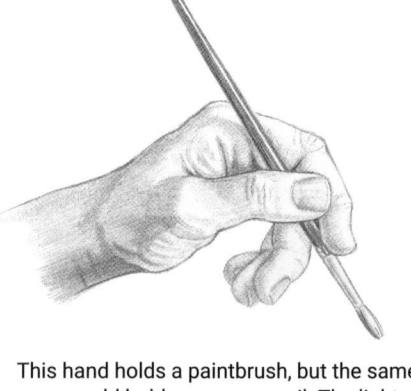

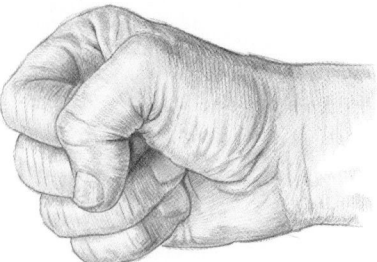

This fist could be holding an object or a tool. The lighting is soft and evenly distributed from a source to the viewer's left.

These hands show the differences between male and female hands. The strong lighting is from above, creating bright highlights on the back of the woman's hand.

Using your hand as a model, draw the three poses shown below: palm facing forward, palm facing forward with slightly tilted fingers, and palm facing down with fingertips forward. Start with basic shapes and then draw the details.

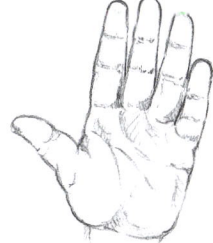

Palm View from Below Hold your hand in the mirror with the palm facing forward. Notice the fingers and palm at their natural size and shape with no foreshortening.

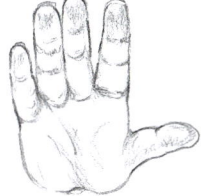

Fingers Tilted Forward Tilt your hand slightly downward. Notice how the palm and fingers become shorter in the mirror.

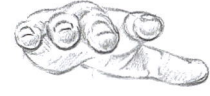

Fingers Facing Forward In this foreshortened view, the fingers look like little stumps. Also note the shape of the fingernails, which are just small ovals.

Hand Step by Step

This wrist and hand are at rest next to a computer keyboard. Practice drawing this natural pose, focusing first on blocking out the basic shape and then developing the details with shading.

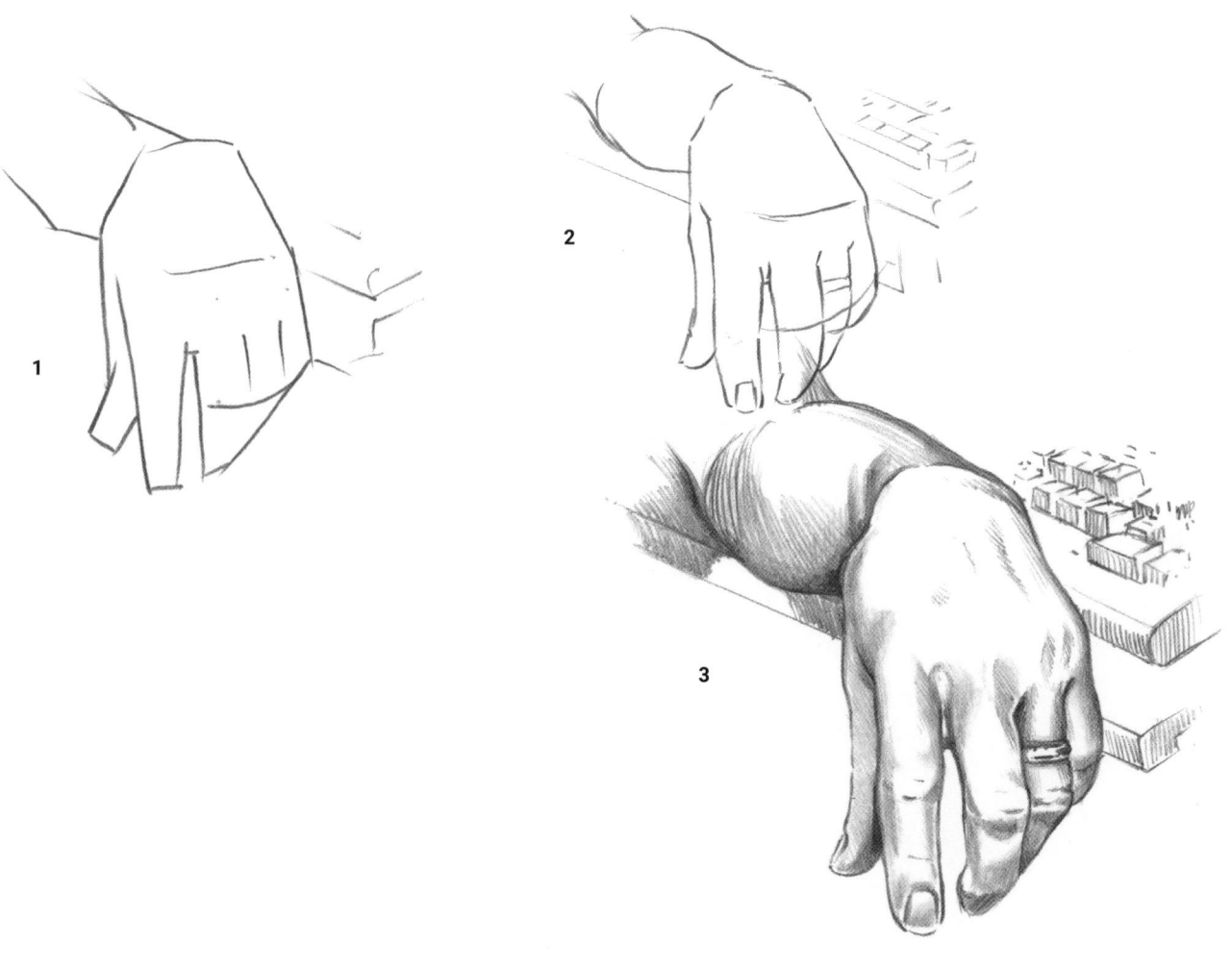

Complete the shading on this hand, paying attention to the natural bends in the arm, wrist, and fingers.

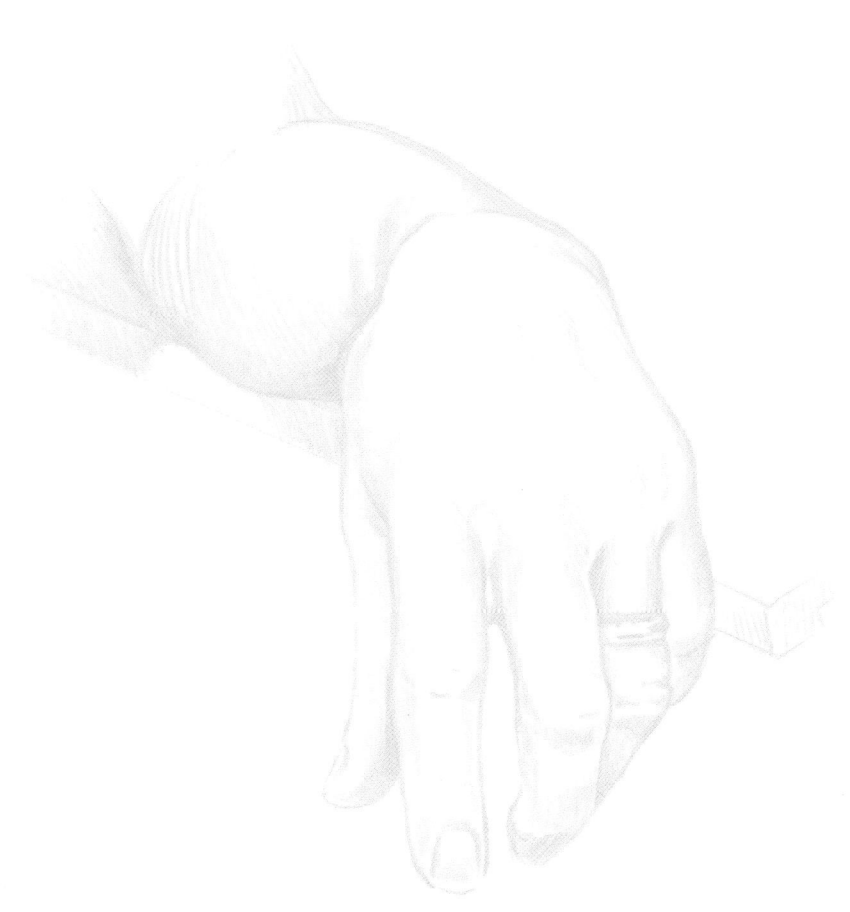

Drawing Feet

Follow the same basic rules for drawing feet as you would for drawing hands. Study the basic shape of the foot and the toes, as well as the overall proportions.

Block in the shape in two parts: The main part of the foot and the toes. Once you've finished the outline, add minimal shading to develop the form.

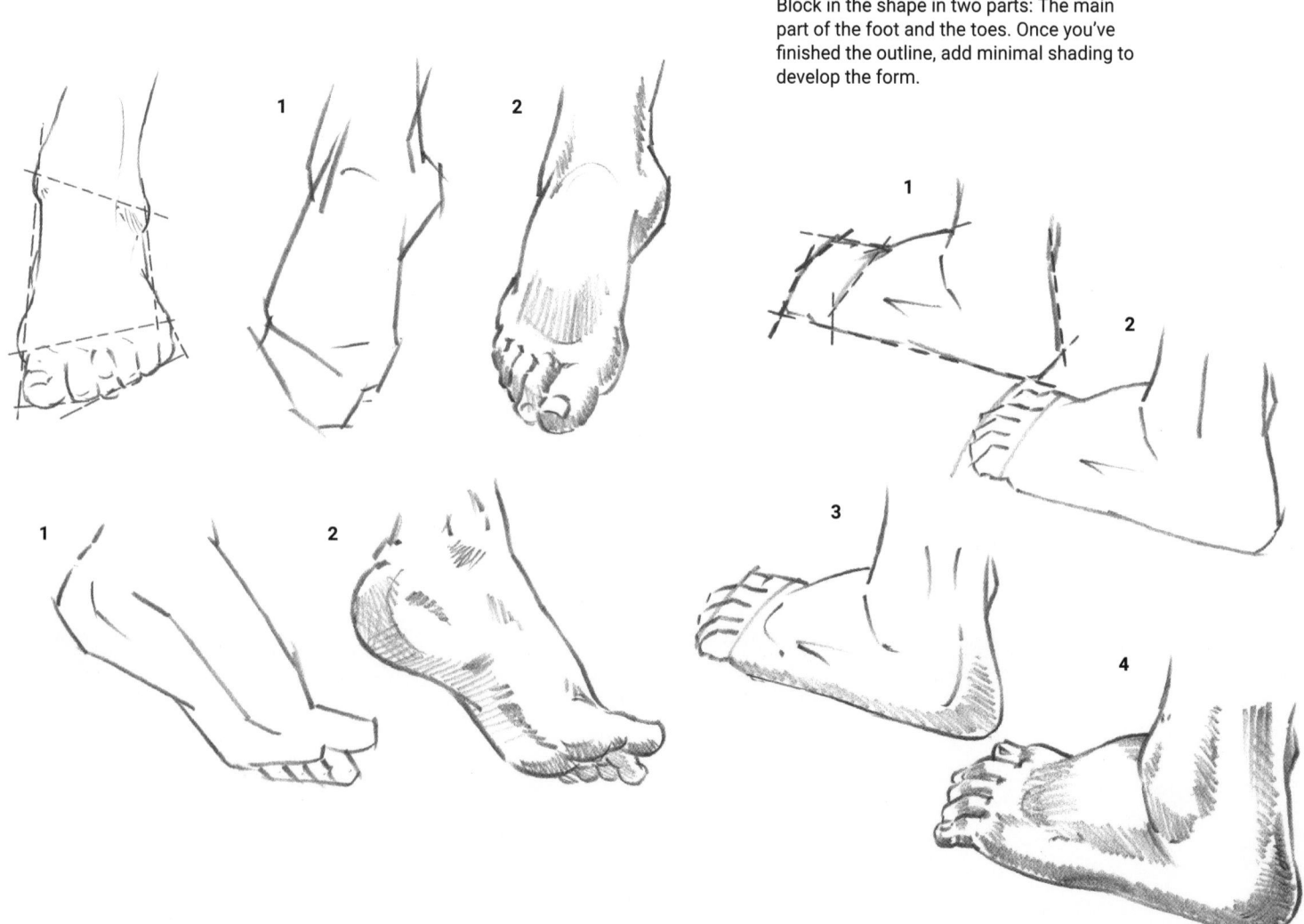

Use this page to practice drawing feet in a variety of positions.

Combining Elements

Incorporating thoughtful details into your drawings can leave a lasting impression on the viewer. In the drawing below, the hand added to this portrait calls forth images of of Rodin's sculpture *The Thinker*. Try out different poses until you find one you want to draw.

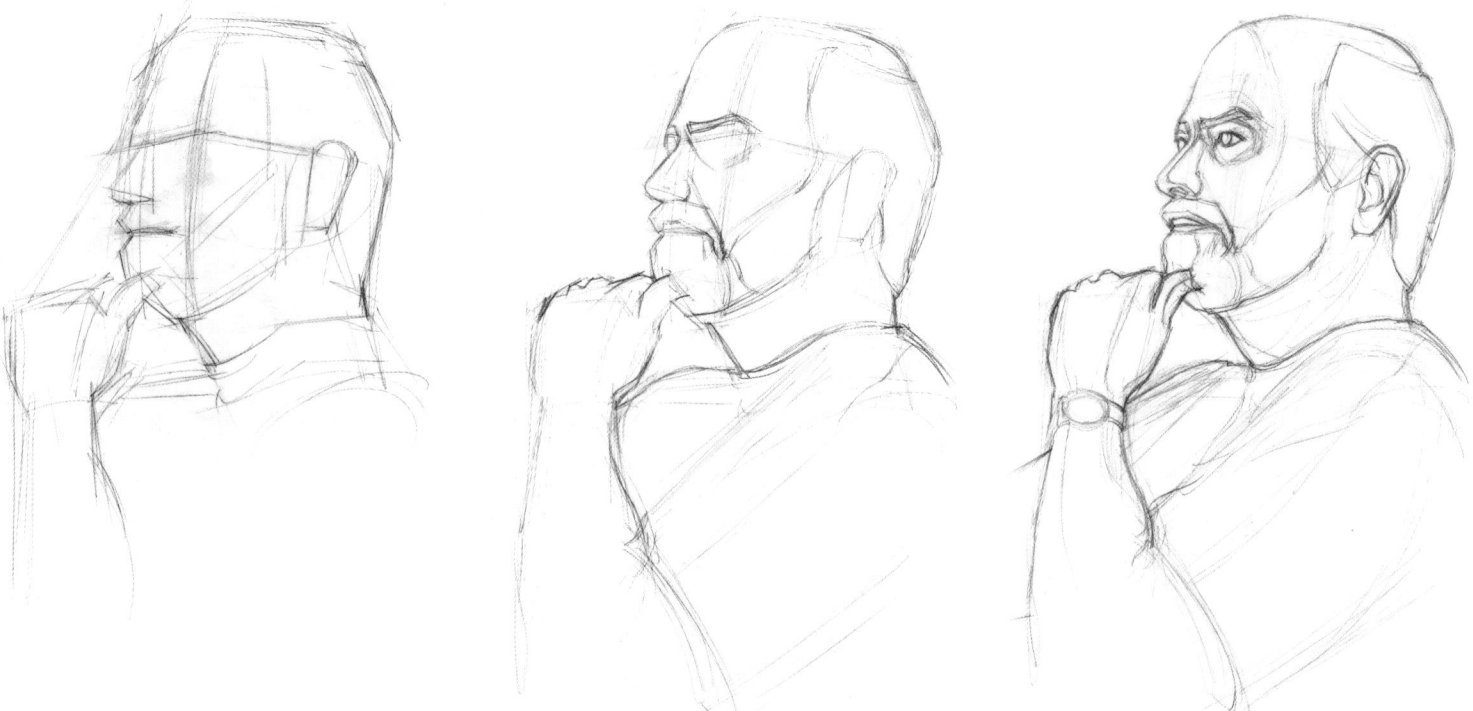

1 First, capture the main planes of the face with simple shapes and lines. Observe carefully how the head position affects the proportions of the face. When drawing the hand, pay attention to its angle to the face.

2 From angular lines, gradually work out the curves of the face. Draw the outlines of the main facial planes with simple strokes before moving on to details. In this three-quarter profile, the averted eye is barely visible.

3 Now, develop the details, including the eye, the eyelids, iris, facial hair, and watch.

Complete the drawing by filling in the shading and highlights.

Establishing Values

Every skin tone is made up of a variety of values. When drawing in pencil, you can accurately capture these differing tones using varying degrees of light and shadow. Before you start drawing, be sure to study your subject to establish the richest darks and brightest lights.

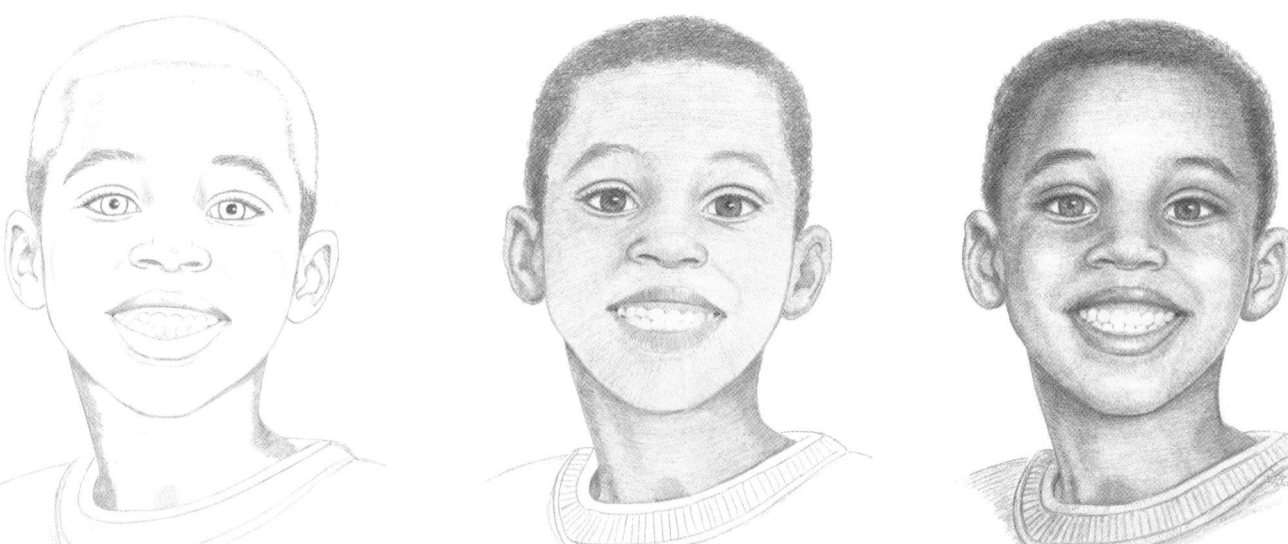

1 Start by sketching the outline of the head and face, placing the features. Using a 2B pencil, sketch in the neck and define the chin. Develop the eyes and use short, quick lines to draw the eyebrows.

2 Shade the nose, neck, and top lip. Using quick, circular strokes, render the short, curly hair. Then detail the eyebrows and eyes.

3 Apply a light layer of shading over the face, always varying the direction of strokes as necessary to follow the shapes of the different planes.

Practice establishing values using the outline below.
Remember to pay attention to the light source, so you can lift out
highlights where appropriate.

Working with Light

Light is crucial to the atmosphere of a drawing. Shadows also depend on light, as they have more or less contrast depending on the lighting. For this drawing, render the face using pencils in varying degrees of hardness and make liberal use of blending stumps to smooth transitions.

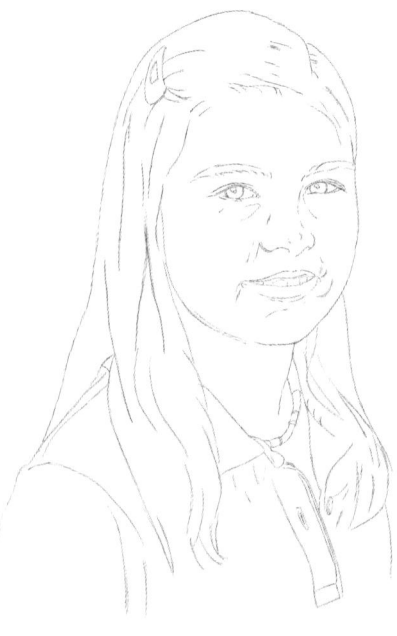 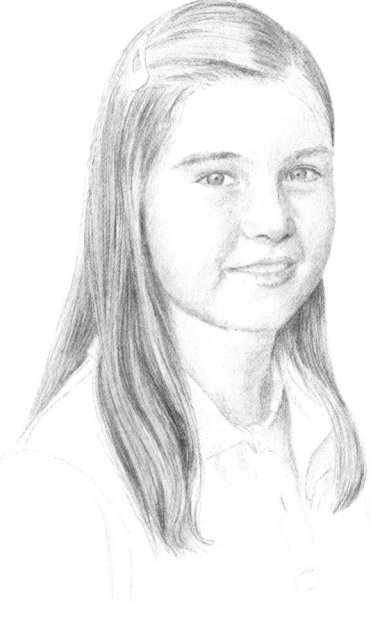 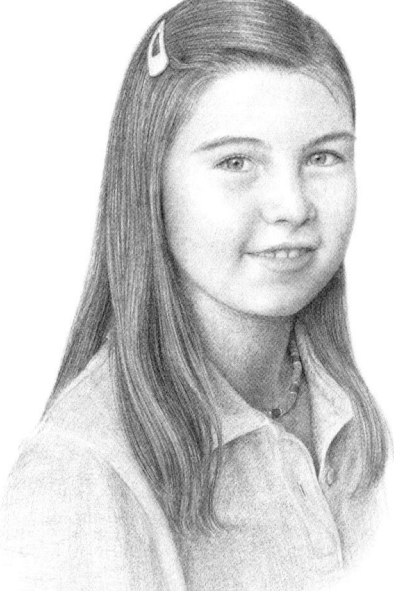

1 Using an HB pencil, outline the basic shape of the head, neck, and hair. Block in the features and the clothing.

2 Using a 2B pencil, draw long strokes for the hair that follow the direction of growth. Add light shading in the iris of each eye. For the face, use light strokes that curve with the shape of cheeks and jaw. Indicate the shadow under the lower lip.

3 Build up the shading of the hair, and use HB and 2H pencils to add light crosshatching in the face to build up the tones. Deepen the upper and lower eyelashes with short lines. Refine the nose and mouth. Lift out highlights using a kneaded eraser and use a blending stump to smooth and soften the shading.

Practice developing light and shadow using the outline provided.
Remember to use a kneaded eraser to lift out highlights.

Developing Hair

There are many different types and styles of hair: thick and thin; long and short; curly, straight, and wavy; and braided. And because hair is often one of an individual's most distinguishing features, knowing how to render different types and textures is essential. When drawing hair, don't try to draw every strand; just create the overall impression and allow the viewer's eye and imagination to fill in the rest.

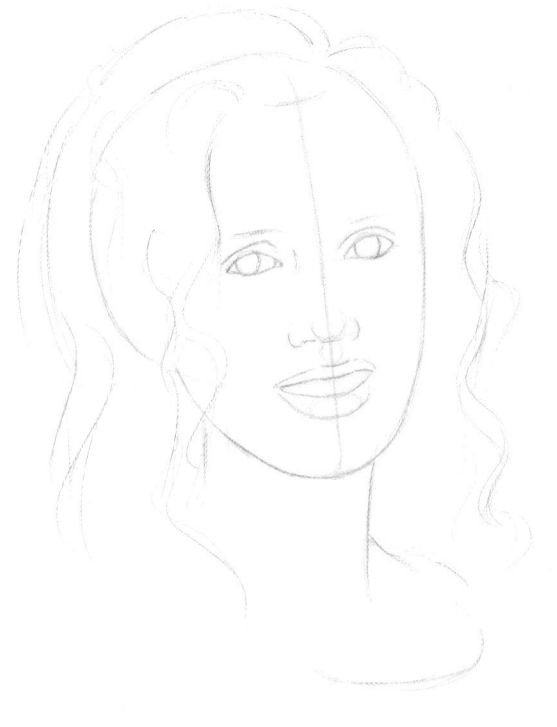

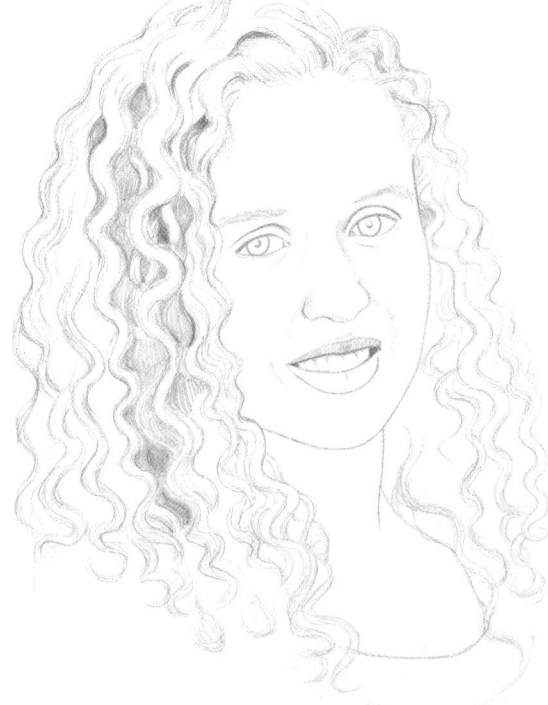

1 Use an HB pencil to sketch the shape of the head and place the features. Then use loose strokes to block in the general outline of the hair. Starting at the part on the left side of the head, lightly draw the hair in the direction of growth on either side of the part. At this stage, merely indicate the shape of the hair; don't worry about the individual ringlets.

2 Switch to a 2B pencil and start refining the eyes, eyebrows, nose, and mouth. Then define the neckline of the shirt with curved lines. Lightly sketch in sections of ringlets, working from top to bottom. Start adding dark values underneath and behind certain sections of hair, creating contrast and depth.

Using a 2B pencil, complete the drawing below
using the outline provided.

Ringlets and Braids

Learning how to draw different types of hair is important if you are going to master drawing people. Start with basic lines in the general shape of the hairstyle. Then layer in strokes a little at a time. Use a kneaded eraser to lift out highlights to give the hair a natural shine.

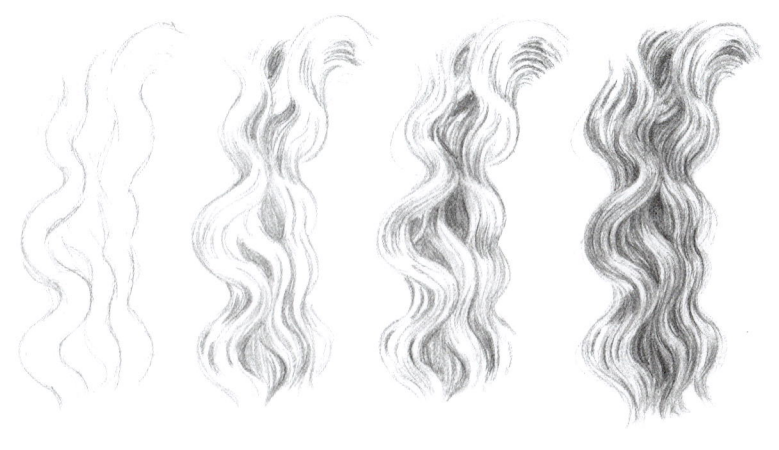

1 Sketch the shapes of the ringlets using curved, S-shaped lines. Make sure to draw them so they are not too similar in shape. Some should be thick and others should be thin.

2 Squint to find the dark and light values of the ringlets. Leave the top of the ringlets (the hair closest to the head) lighter and add a bit more shading as you move down the strands, indicating that the light is coming from above.

3 To create the darkest values underneath the hair, place the strokes closer together.

4 Add even darker values, making sure that your transitions are smooth and that there are no abrupt changes in direction.

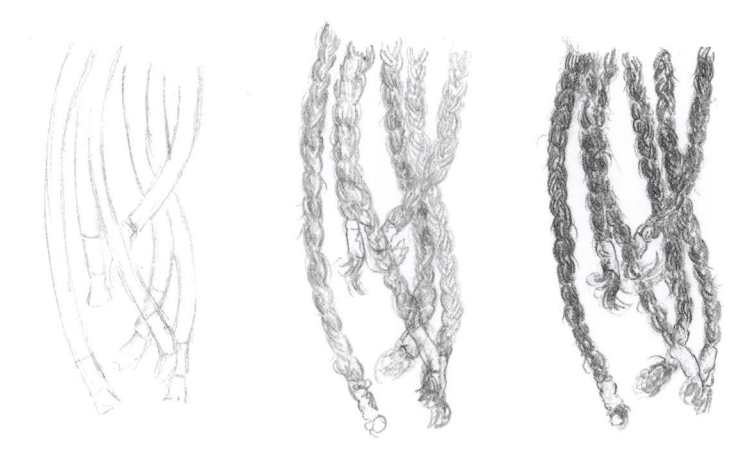

1 Sketch the outline of each braid. Taper the ends a bit, adding a line across the bottom of each to indicate the ties that hold the braids together.

2 Start shading each section, indicating the overlapping hair in each braid. Add some wispy hair around the braids to add realism.

3 Continue shading the braids using heavier strokes. Add more wisps of hair. Use a kneaded eraser to pull out highlights at the bottom of each braid to denote the ties. To finish, lift out some highlights in the braids themselves.

Practice drawing ringlets, braids, and straight hair using the outlines below.
Use the rest of the page to draw other hair textures.

Drawing Facial Hair

Facial hair is another characteristic that distinguishes one individual from the next. Short, dark strokes are perfect for rendering a thick, coarse beard; whereas light, sweeping strokes are ideal for depicting a wispy mustache. Experiment with variations of light and dark lines when drawing a "salt-and-pepper" beard, and use a series of quick, short lines when indicating stubble.

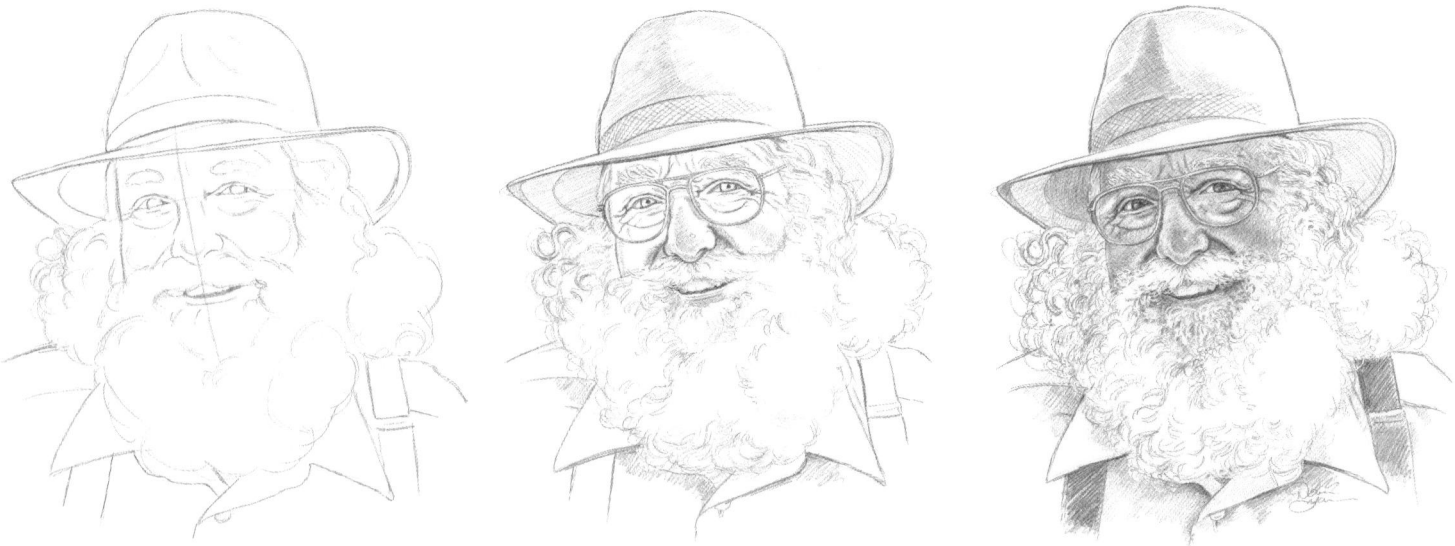

1 Sketch the face with an HB pencil, placing guidelines for the features. Draw the hat and block in the hair, mustache, and beard with loose, curved lines.

2 Add the glasses and continue to define the remaining facial details. Begin shading the tight curls of the beard and mustache. Add darker values to the left side of the face to show the cast shadow of the hat.

3 Add a layer of shading to the irises, leaving white highlights in each eye. Using the edge of a kneaded eraser, lift out a highlight on each lens of the glasses to show the reflected light. Apply more shading to the hat, suspenders, and shirt.

When drawing a face that is partly hidden by facial hair, it is important to draw the entire head and face. This is called "drawing through." After you've established the features, you can add the hair, beard, and accessories.

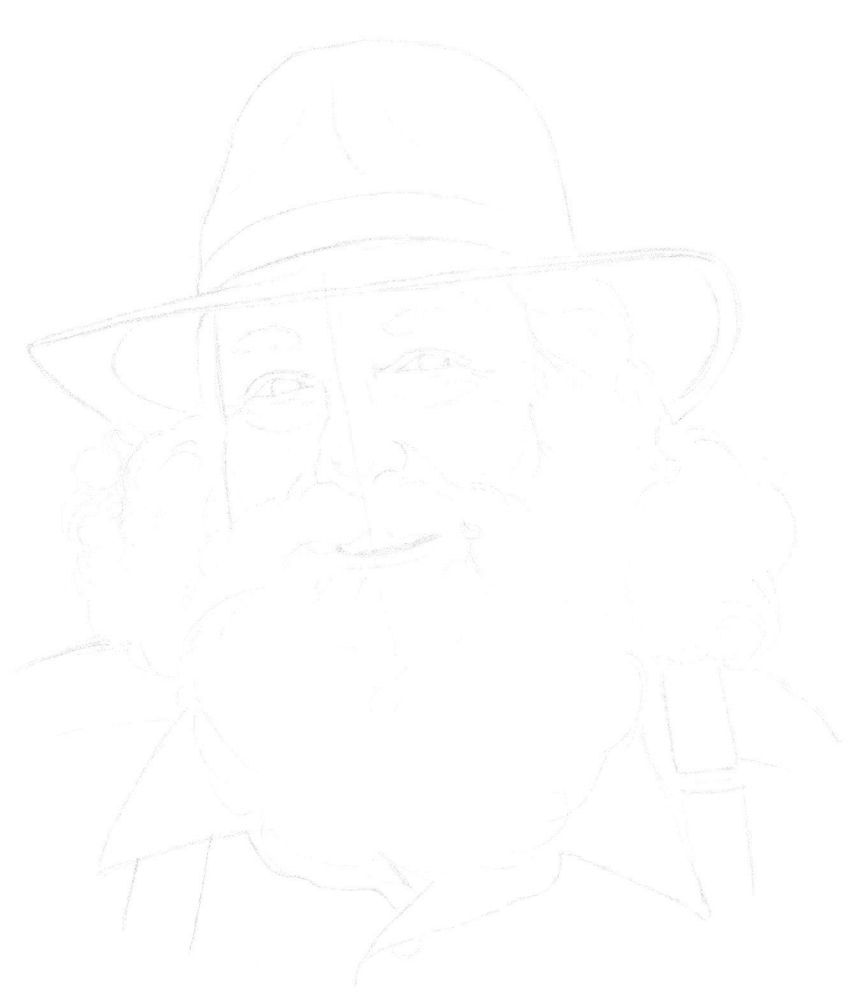

Capturing Emotion

Drawing a wide range of different facial expressions and emotions, especially extreme ones, can be quite enjoyable. Because these are just studies and not formal portraits, draw loosely to add energy and a look of spontaneity—as if a camera had captured the face at just that moment.

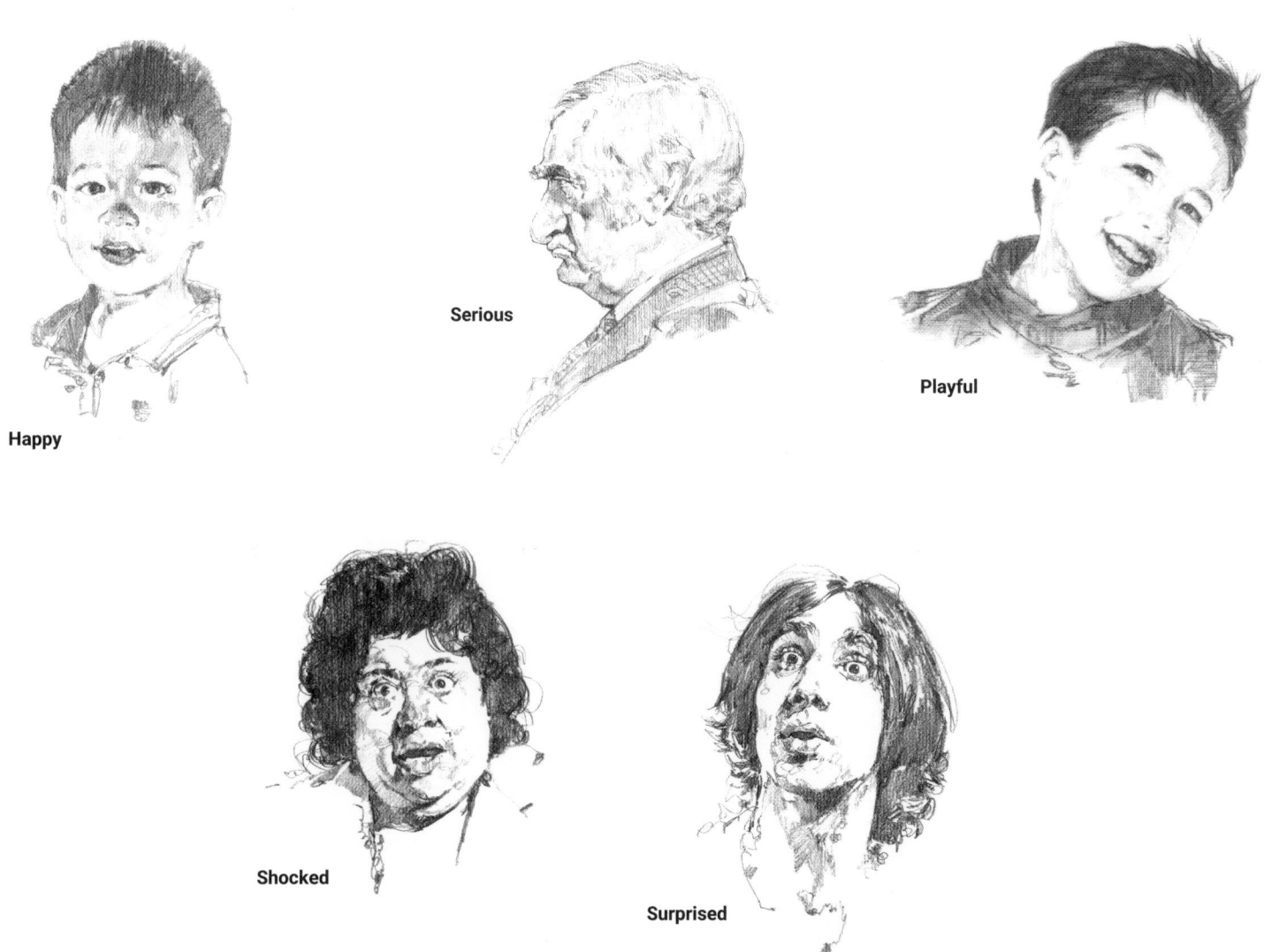

Happy

Serious

Playful

Shocked

Surprised

Now that you know how to draw facial features,
try drawing some different facial expressions.

Basic Perspective

The rules of perspective are guides for keeping objects and people in proper proportion to one another in a composition. Mastering perspective will add realism to your drawings. First, establish the horizon line and the vanishing points. Any figures drawn along these lines will be in proper perspective.

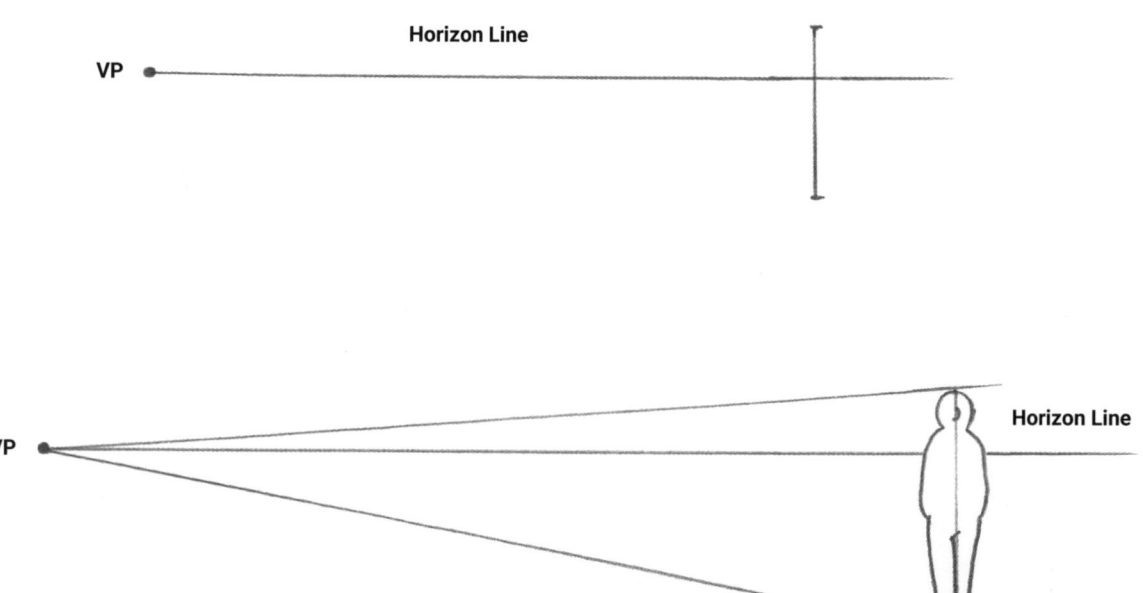

Horizon Line the line that represents the viewer's eye level.

Vanishing Point (VP) the point on the horizon line where parallel lines, such as railroad tracks, appear to meet or converge.

People in Perspective

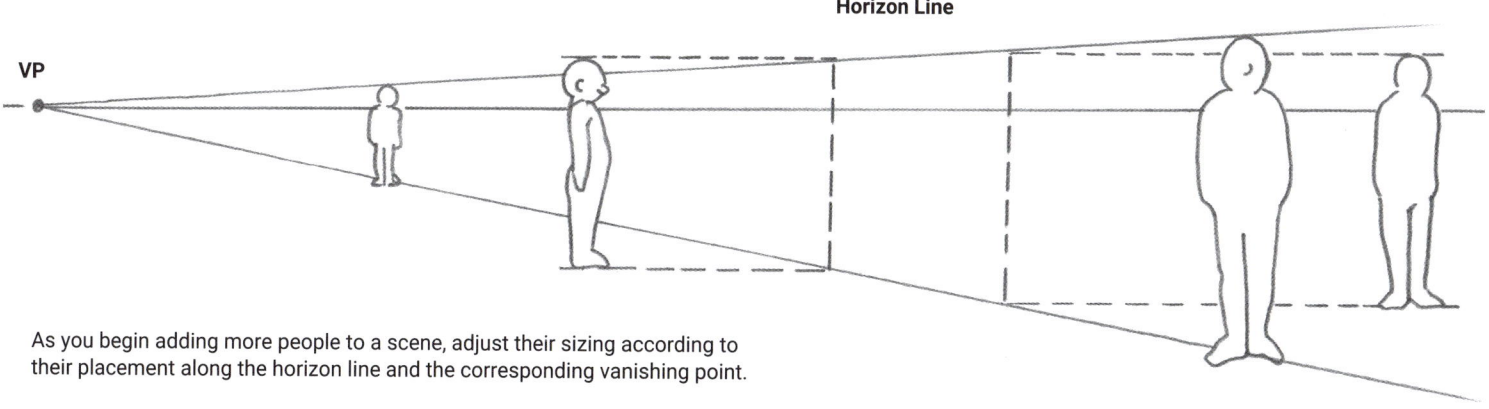

Horizon Line

VP

As you begin adding more people to a scene, adjust their sizing according to their placement along the horizon line and the corresponding vanishing point.

Use the space below to practice the basic principles of perspective.

Size and Depth

This illustration shows many heads in perspective. Imagine they are spectators at a concert or in a movie theater. Start by establishing your vanishing point at eye level. Then draw one head representing the person closest to you, and use it as a reference for determining the sizes of the other figures in the drawing.

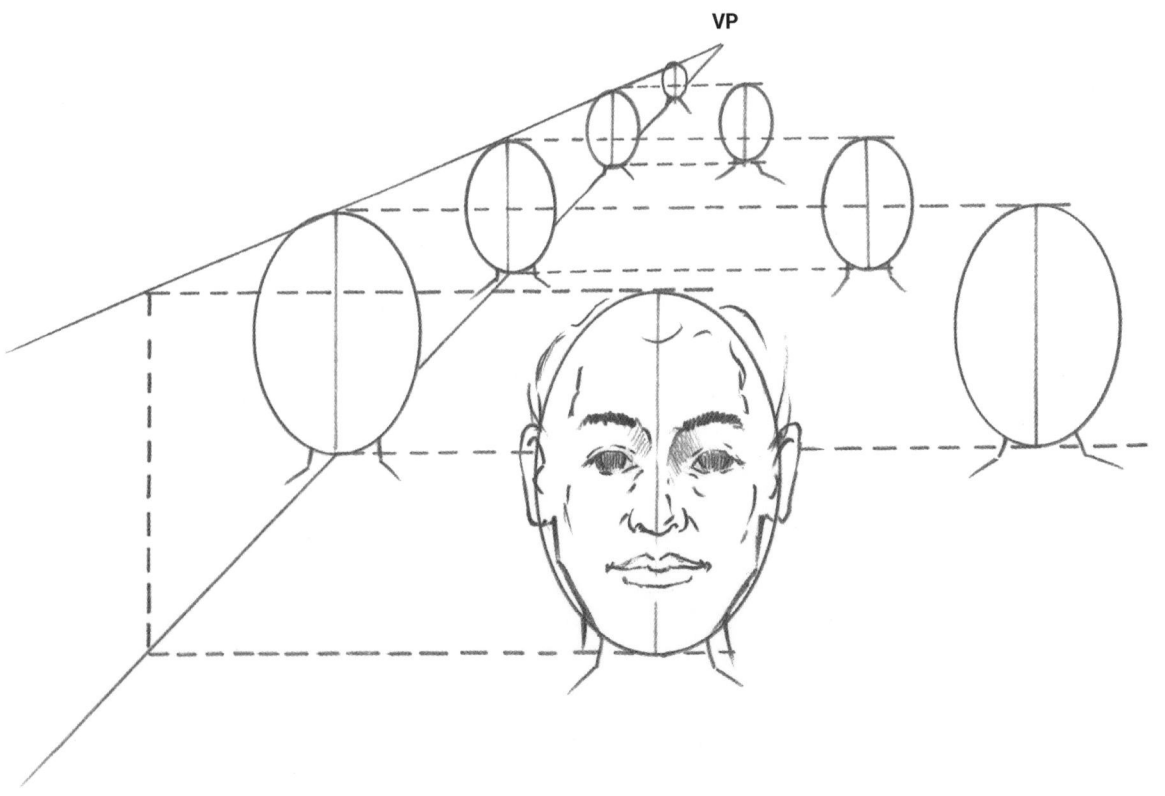

Fill in the right side of the template below with a frontal
view of heads in perspective.

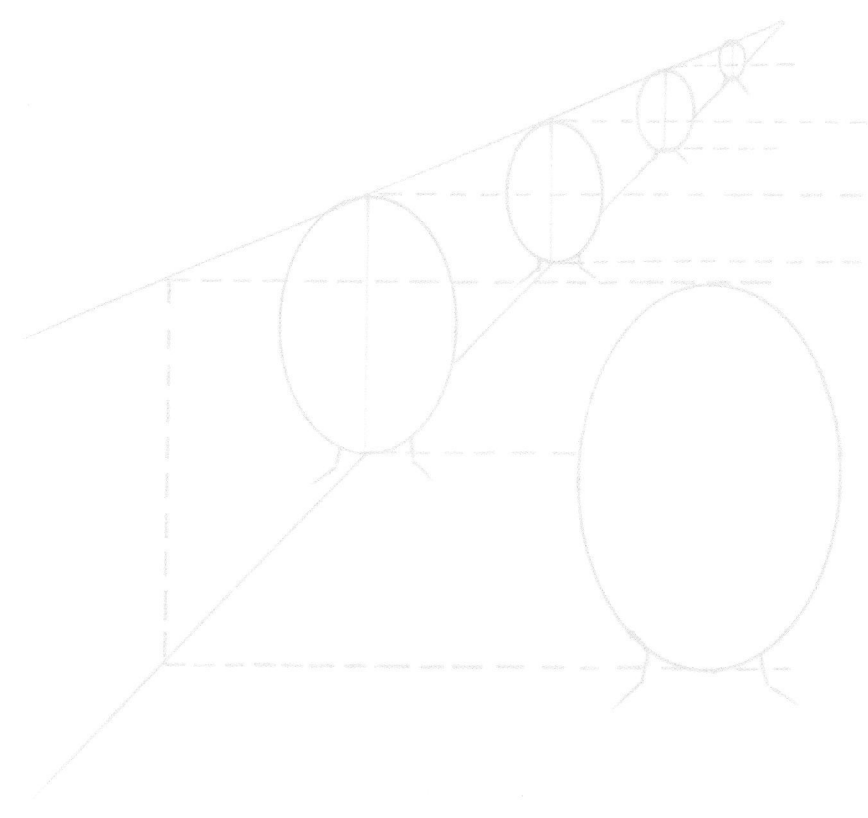

Drawing Full Figures

Placing full figures in a scene follows the same rules of perspective. The illustration below features entire figures aligned with one vanishing point, but as scenes get more complex, you can have two or even three vanishing points.

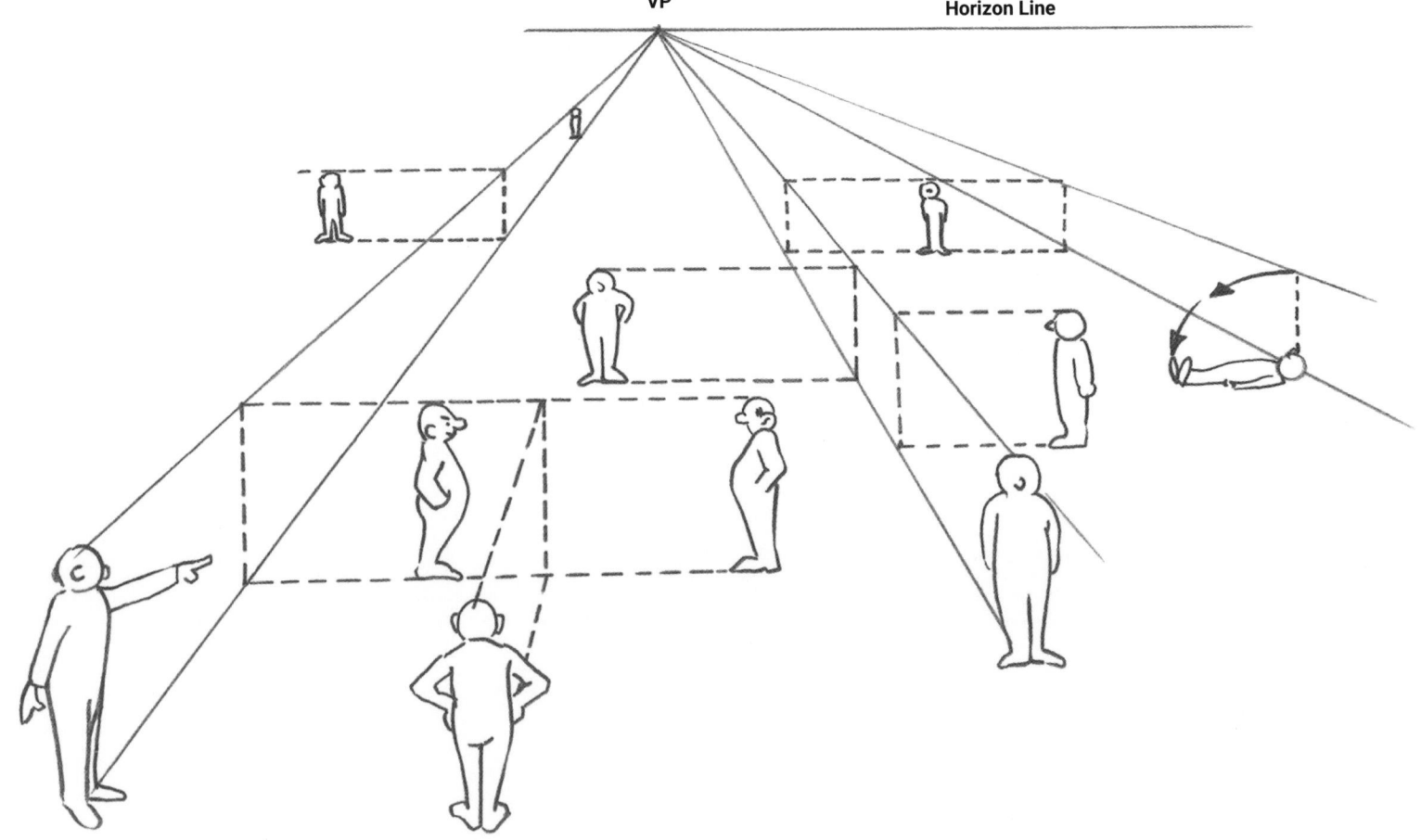

Practice drawing multiple people in perspective
using the template provided.

Complete Figures

Creating a composition that shows a complete person can be challenging. A standing figure is much taller than it is wide, so the figure should be positioned so that its action relates naturally to the eye level of the viewer and the horizon line. To place more than one figure on the picture plane, use the rules of perspective.

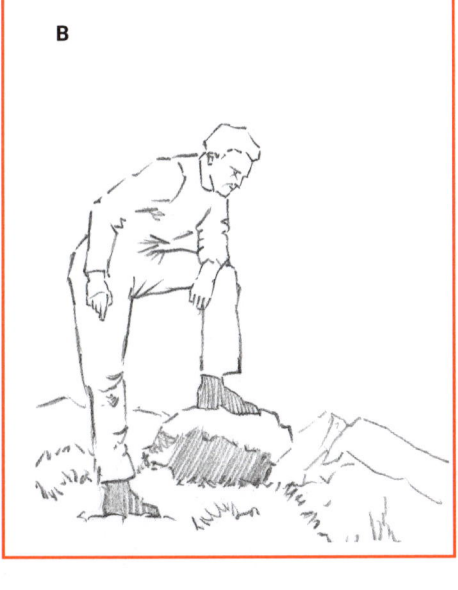

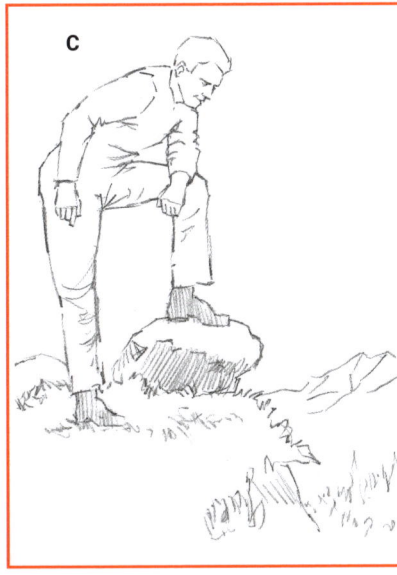

Full Figure Placement In image A, the subject is too perfectly centered in the picture plane. In image B, the figure is placed too far to the left. Image C is an example of effective placement of a human figure in a composition.

Trace the outline below to develop a sense of
balanced composition. Then draw the composition
on your own in the box provided.

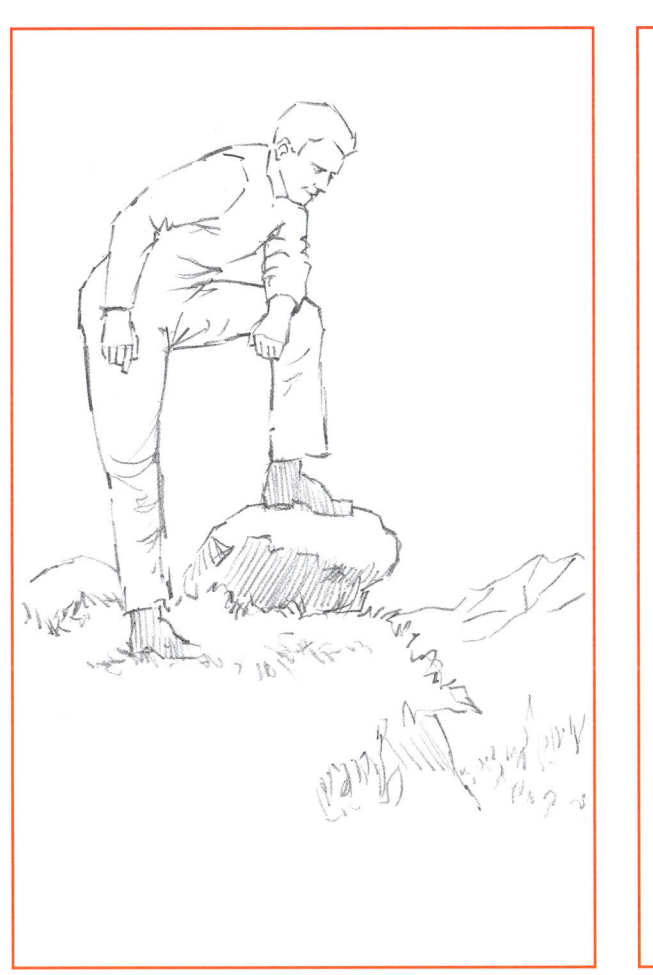

Individuals and Groups

Experienced artists reduce figures to basic geometric shapes when composing a drawing. Over time, you will develop an eye for the geometric shapes that individuals or groups form. Think about how you want to construct the picture and draw a rough sketch. The following example shows how to construct the complex image, starting with the shapes of the main image elements.

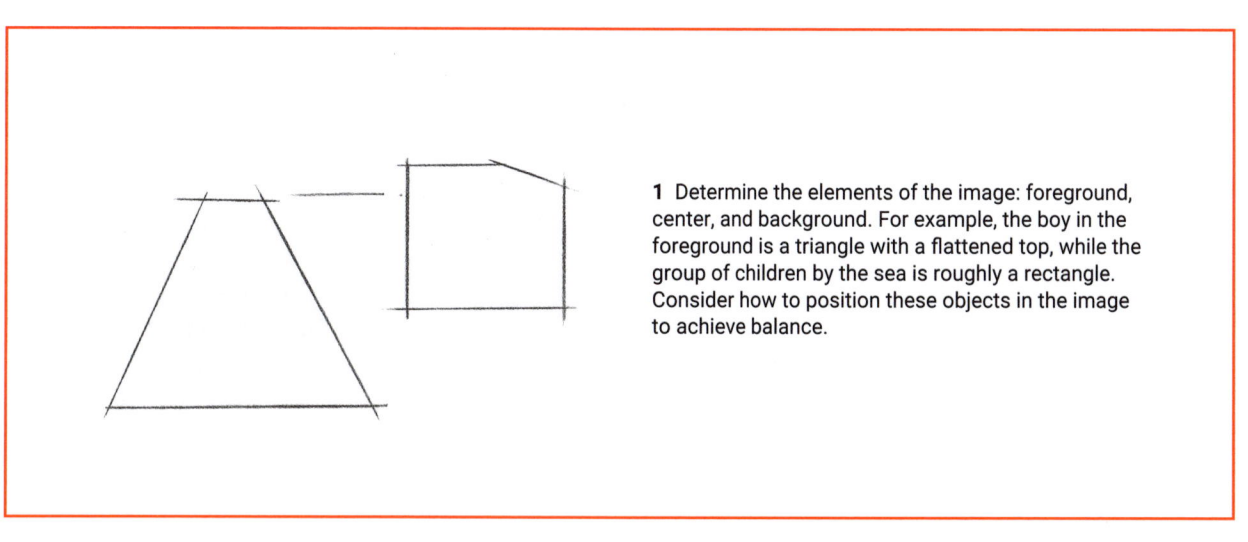

1 Determine the elements of the image: foreground, center, and background. For example, the boy in the foreground is a triangle with a flattened top, while the group of children by the sea is roughly a rectangle. Consider how to position these objects in the image to achieve balance.

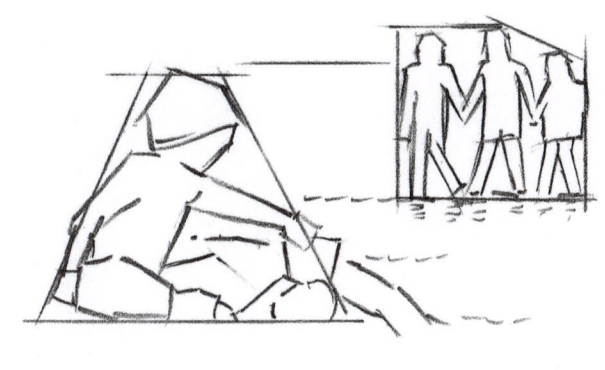

2 Now outline the figures. The little boy with the shovel and bucket takes up a large area in the foreground. The three children by the water are only slightly smaller together. The edge of the sea guides the eye from one main area to the other.

What do you like about the composition below? Are there things that you would change? Trace the details that help make it appear balanced.

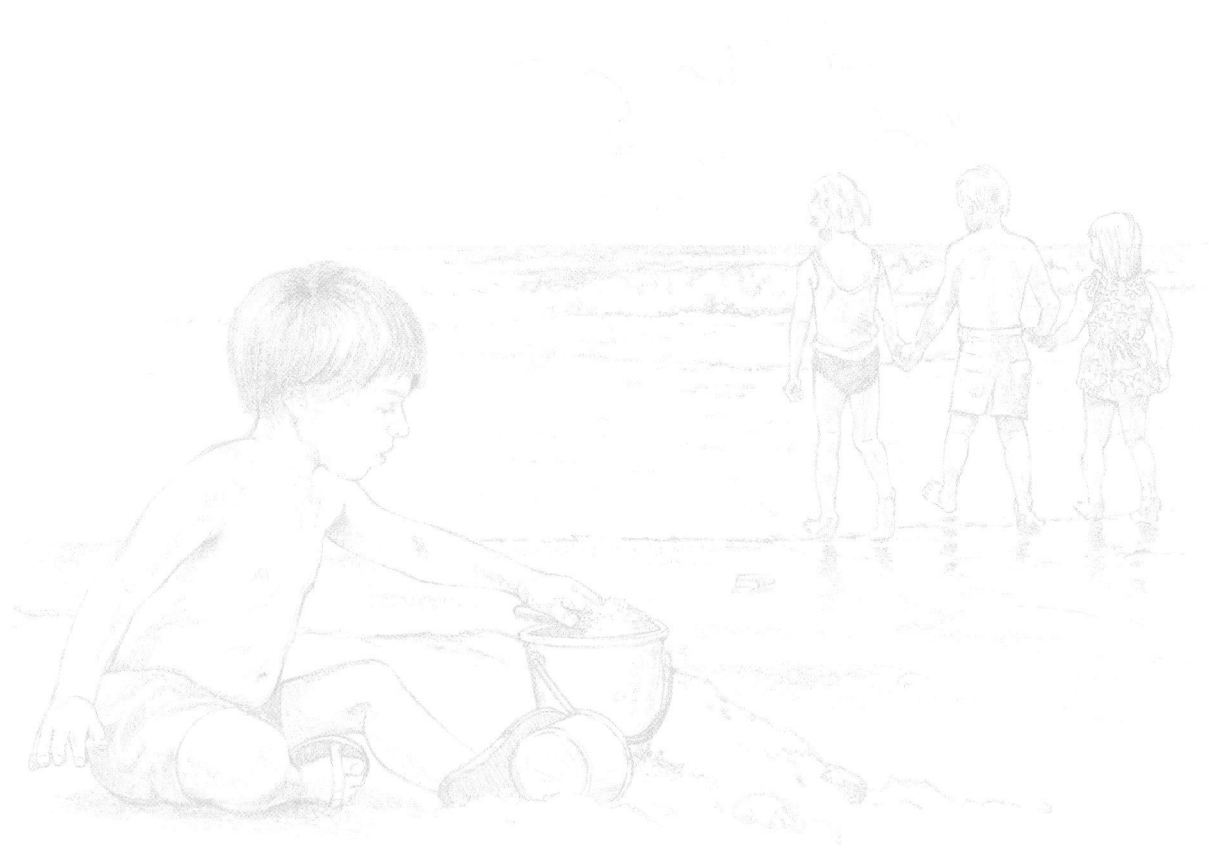

Using References

Using references is a great way to find unique subjects to draw. Balanced, natural poses make for more interesting drawings, as opposed to overly stiff or highly curated poses. Ideally, your subject should appear relaxed and in a pose that reveals their personality.

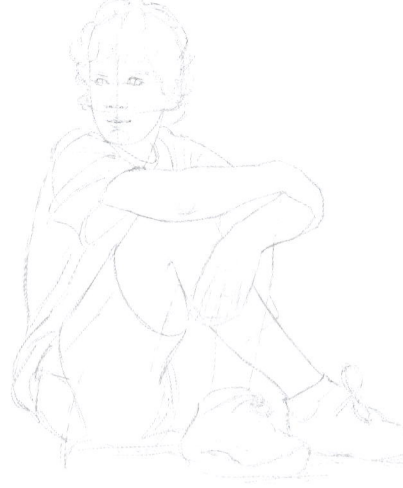

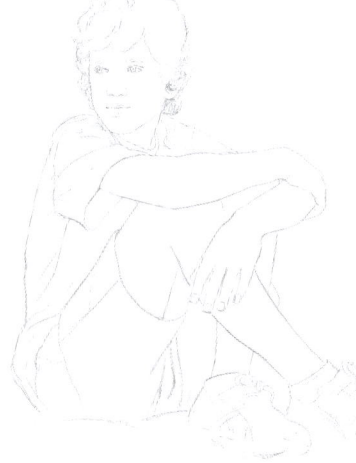

This photo captures the subject in a relaxed position. The head position adds interest to the pose.

1 Establish guidelines and place the facial features, referring to the photo as you draw. Indicate the basic shapes of the figure.

2 Use a B pencil to refine the facial features and the hair. Refine the shapes of the hands, arms, legs, and clothing, removing unneeded lines with a kneaded eraser.

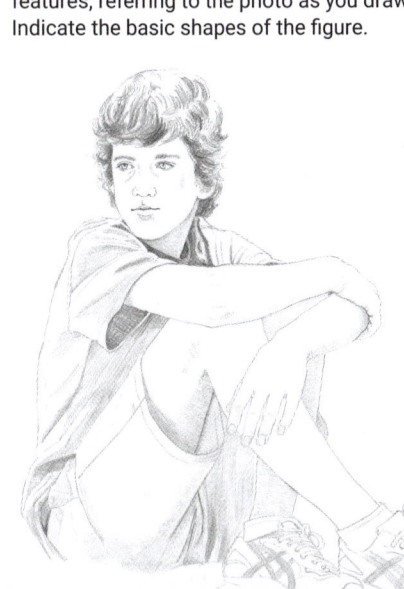

3 Using a 2B pencil, shade the hair with strokes that follow the direction of growth. Add shading around the eyes, cheekbones, lips, and neck. Use a sharp pencil and small strokes for the eyebrows and lashes. Add more shading to the clothing and shoes, rendering additional details as you go.

Complete the drawing you started on the previous page.
Shade the form using a 2B pencil and light pressure. Use a 3B pencil
to shade some of the darker areas. Add some grass to the scene.

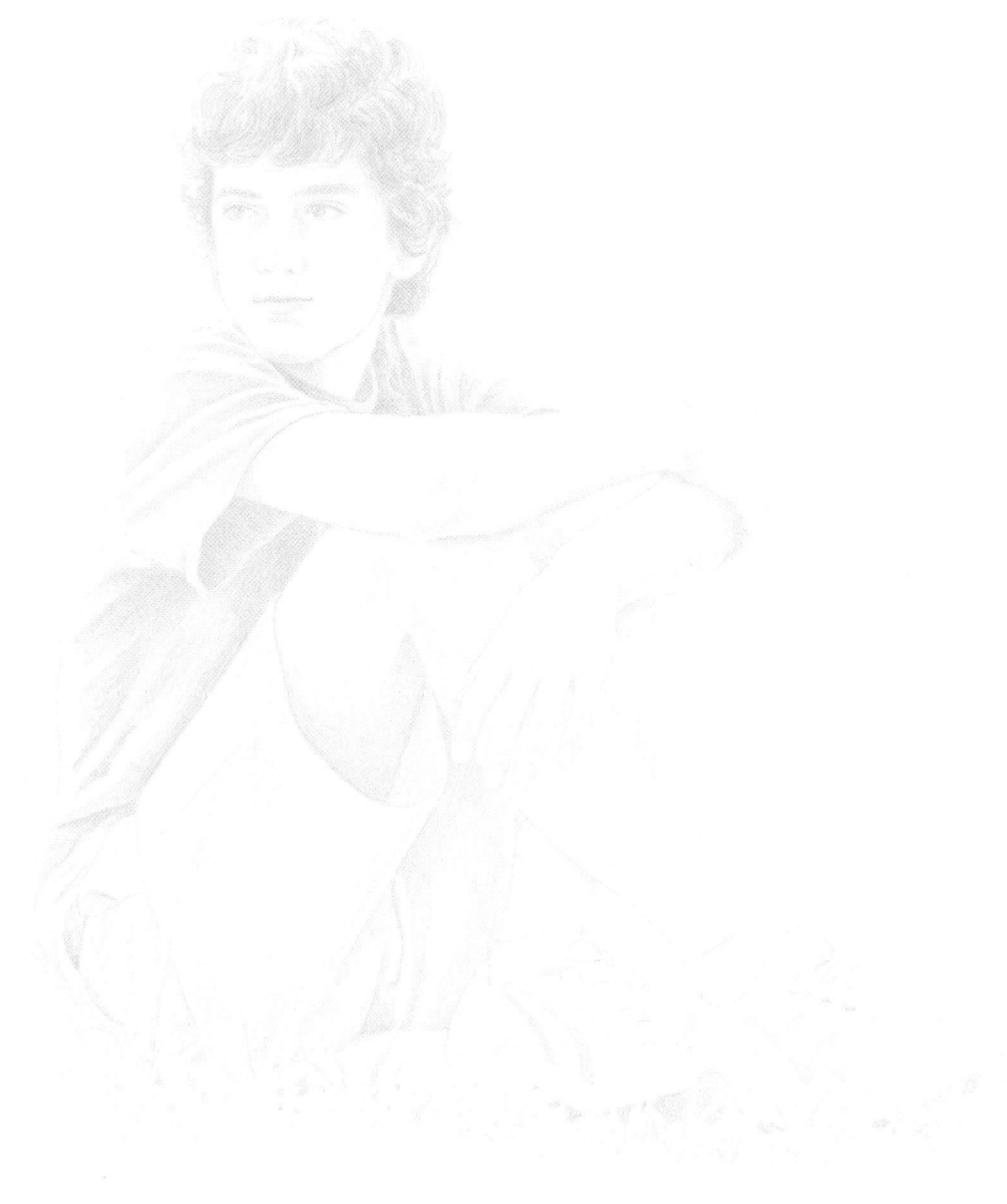

Choosing a Pose

When taking portraits of children, avoid working with just one photo. Instead, use a small collection of shots, showing the subject positioned in different angles and in various types of lighting. Then feel free to combine the different points to create a new composition in your drawing.

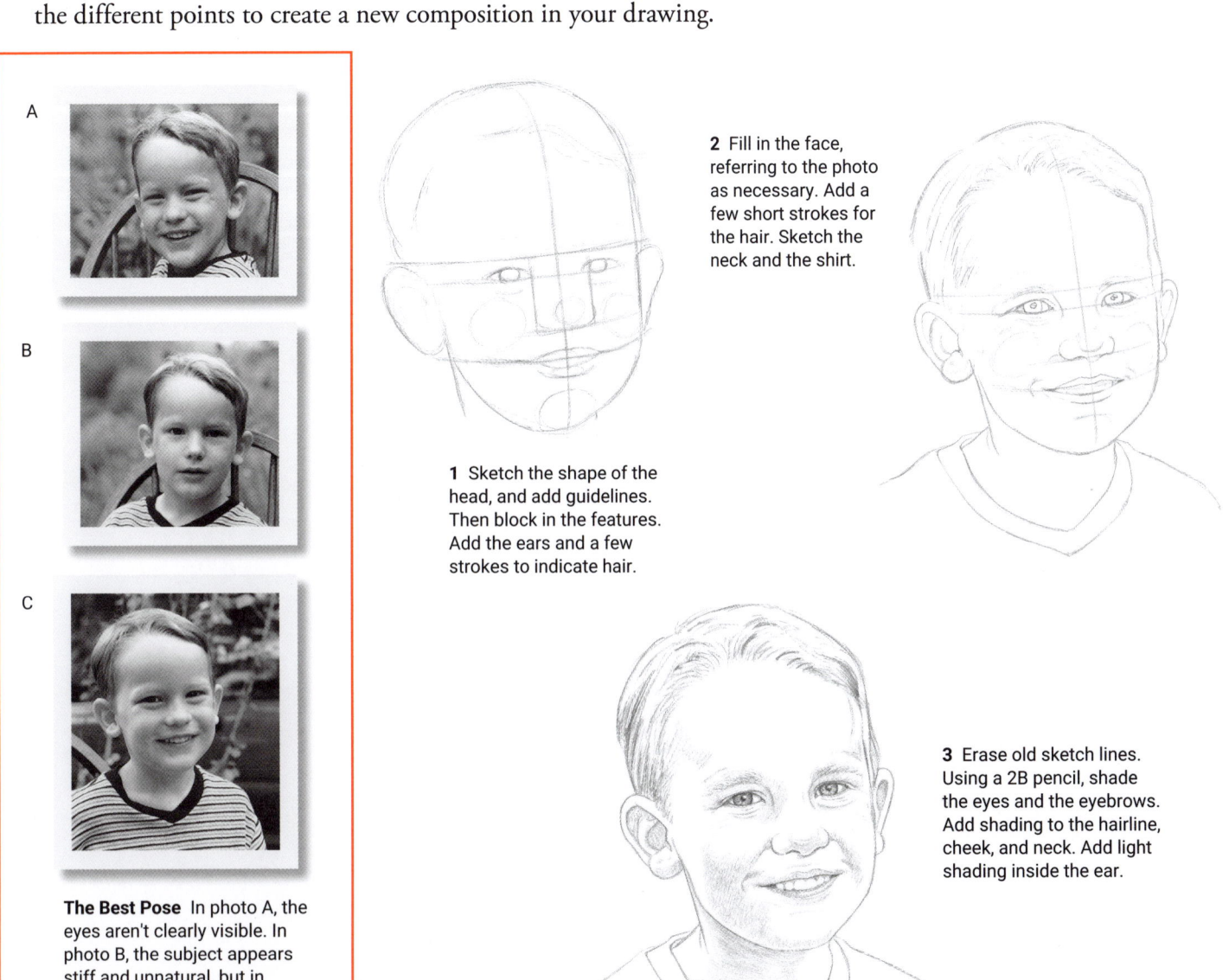

A

B

C

The Best Pose In photo A, the eyes aren't clearly visible. In photo B, the subject appears stiff and unnatural, but in photo C, the expression and pose are perfect!

1 Sketch the shape of the head, and add guidelines. Then block in the features. Add the ears and a few strokes to indicate hair.

2 Fill in the face, referring to the photo as necessary. Add a few short strokes for the hair. Sketch the neck and the shirt.

3 Erase old sketch lines. Using a 2B pencil, shade the eyes and the eyebrows. Add shading to the hairline, cheek, and neck. Add light shading inside the ear.

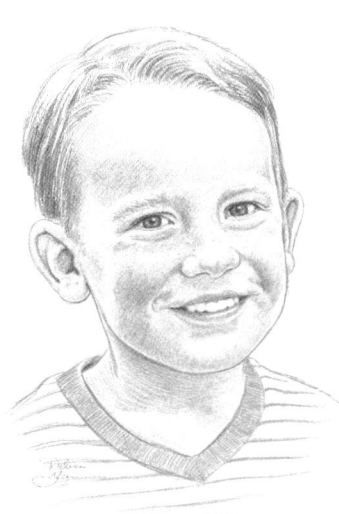

Now it's your turn! Try drawing this portrait on your own using the photos and step-by-step instructions above to help you. Erase the guidelines as you go. Use a 6B pencil for darker lines and darker shading.

Movement and Balance

Another way to make drawings more realistic is to draw the figures in action. Since people hardly ever sit or stand still, your figure drawings of them shouldn't either. You can begin by using simple sketch lines to lay out the dominant action of the figure. Another way to make drawings more realistic is to draw the figures in action.

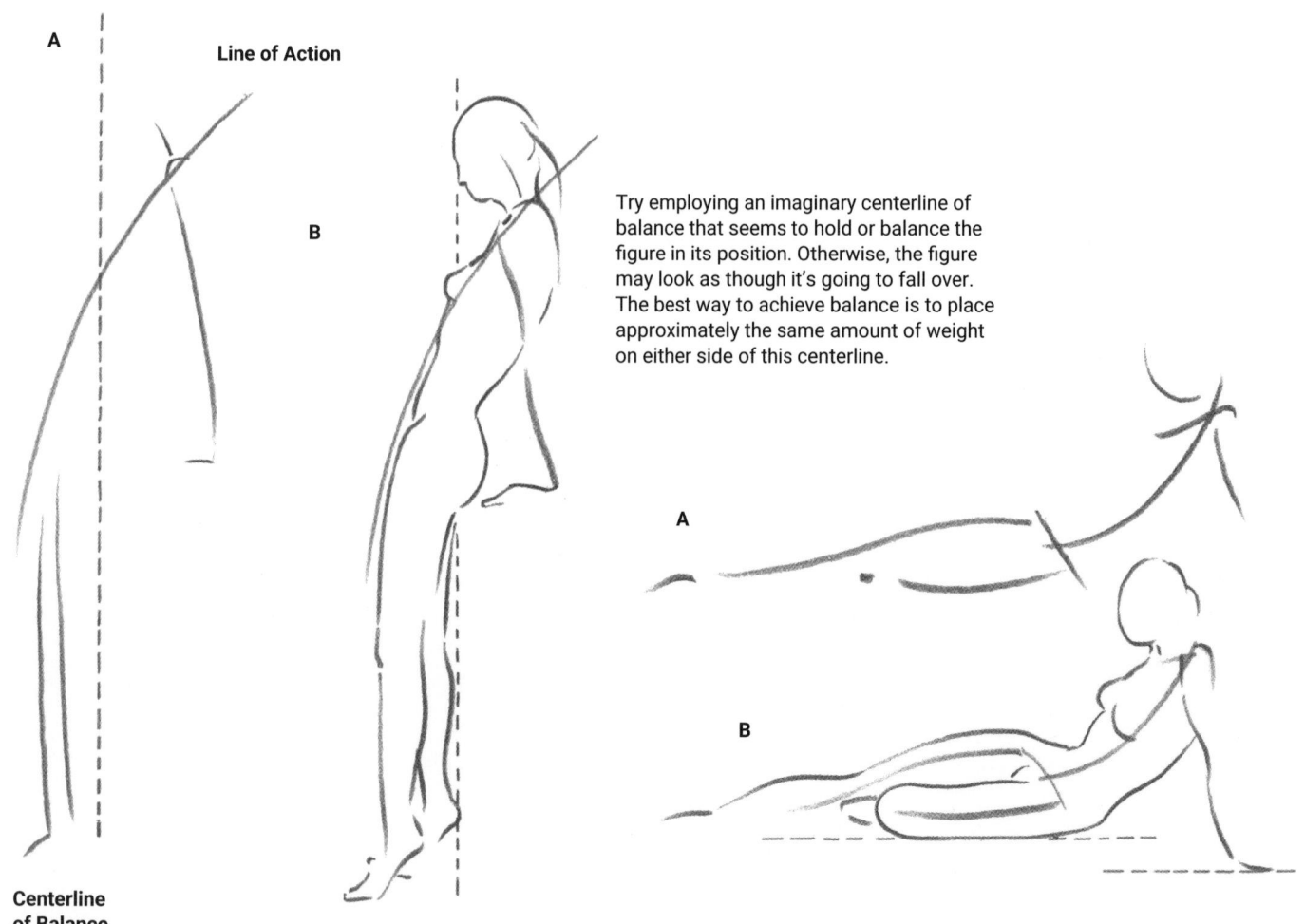

Line of Action

Try employing an imaginary centerline of balance that seems to hold or balance the figure in its position. Otherwise, the figure may look as though it's going to fall over. The best way to achieve balance is to place approximately the same amount of weight on either side of this centerline.

Centerline of Balance

Using both the centerline of
balance and the line of action
help establish effective action
figure drawings.

Try to draw the balance line and
the action line for each of these
examples.

Figures in Motion

To draw a moving figure, begin by drawing the action line. Then, build the rest of the figure around that line, paying careful attention to the way the body maintains its balance.

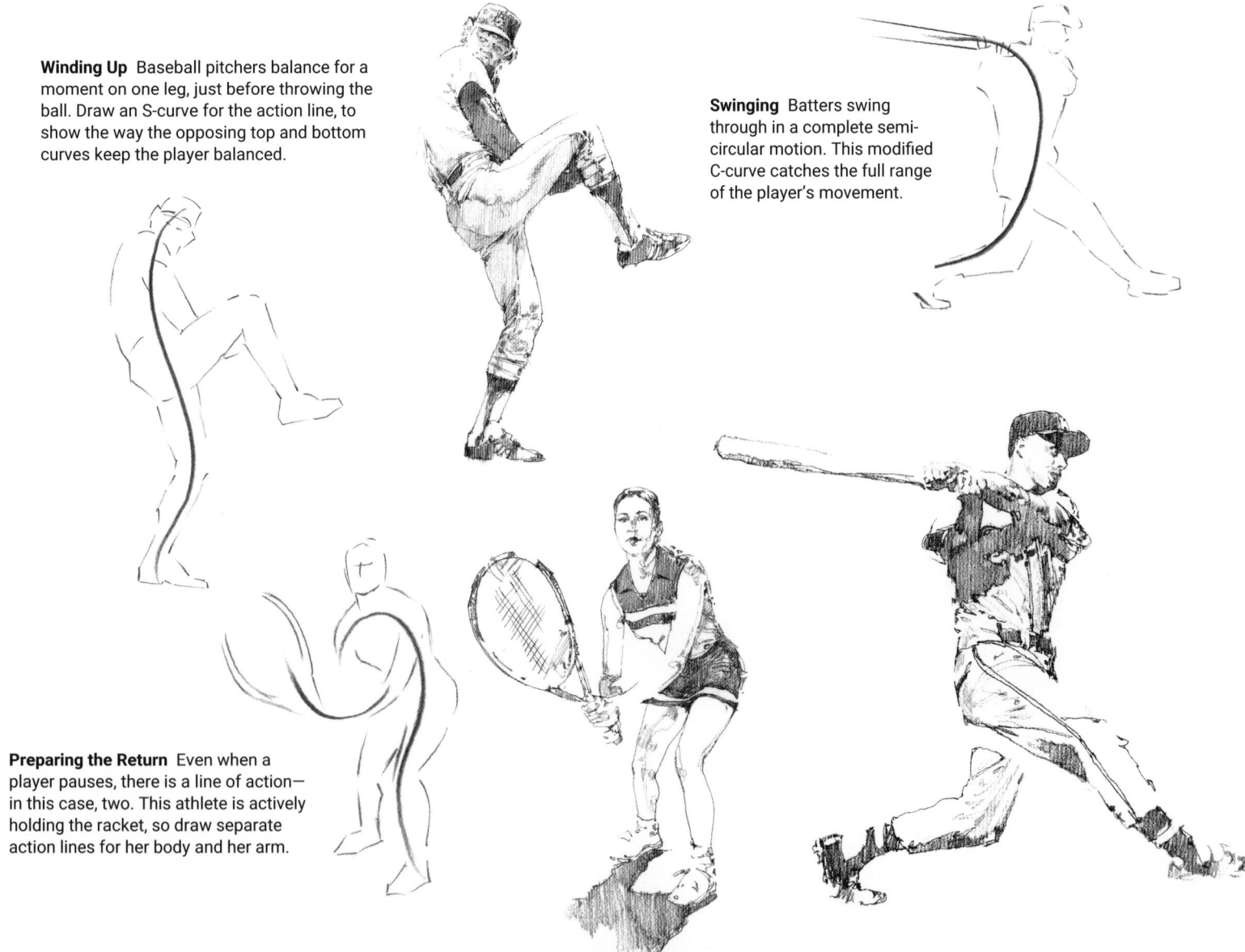

Winding Up Baseball pitchers balance for a moment on one leg, just before throwing the ball. Draw an S-curve for the action line, to show the way the opposing top and bottom curves keep the player balanced.

Swinging Batters swing through in a complete semi-circular motion. This modified C-curve catches the full range of the player's movement.

Preparing the Return Even when a player pauses, there is a line of action—in this case, two. This athlete is actively holding the racket, so draw separate action lines for her body and her arm.

To draw figures in motion, start with simple stick figures
and then add ovals and circles to fill out the forms.

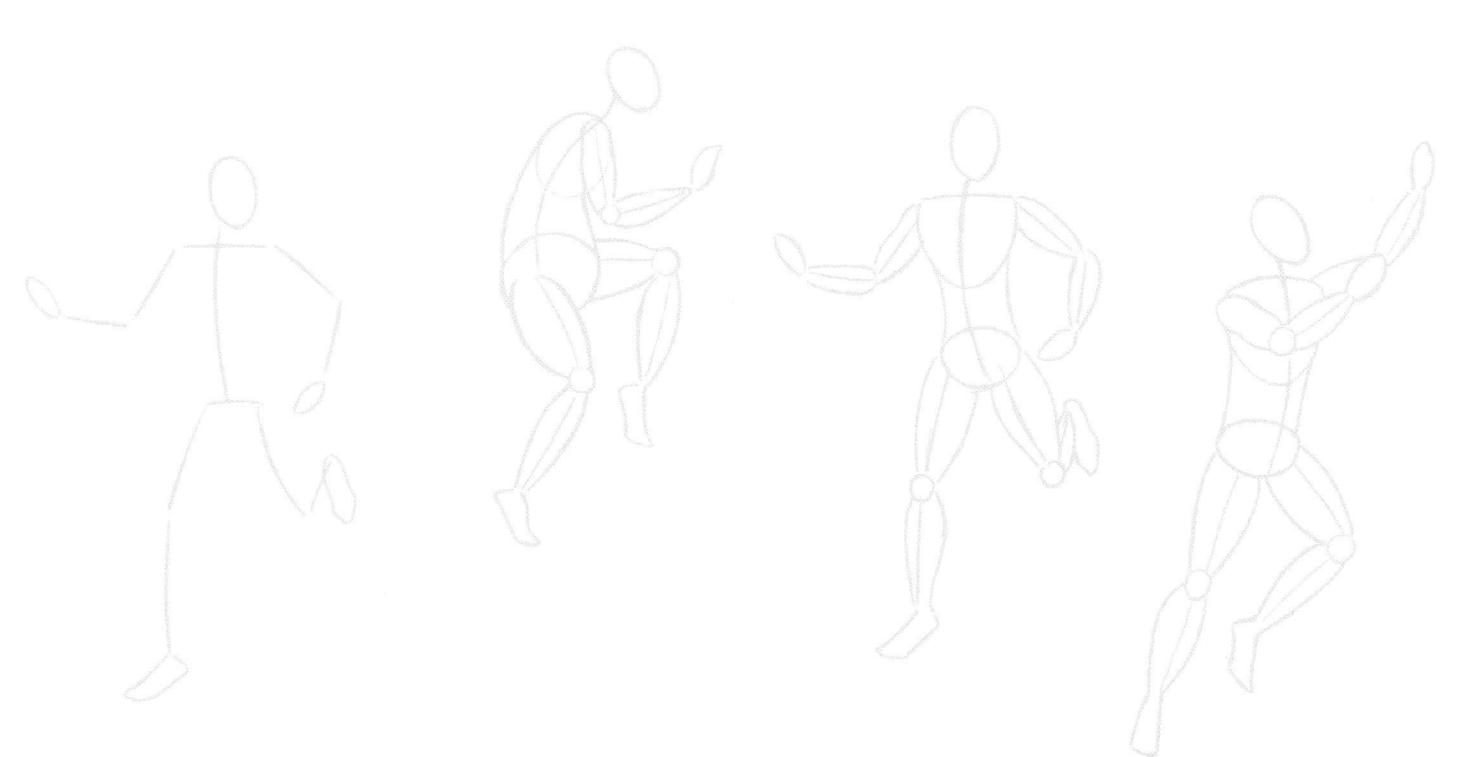

Action Poses

To draw figures in action, it's helpful to start with gesture drawings. First determine the main thrust of the movement, from the head, down the spine, and through the legs; this is the *line of action*. Then briefly sketch the general shapes of the figure around this line. These quick sketches are great for practicing drawing figures in action and sharpening your powers of observation. Once you compile a series of gesture drawings, you can combine them into a scene.

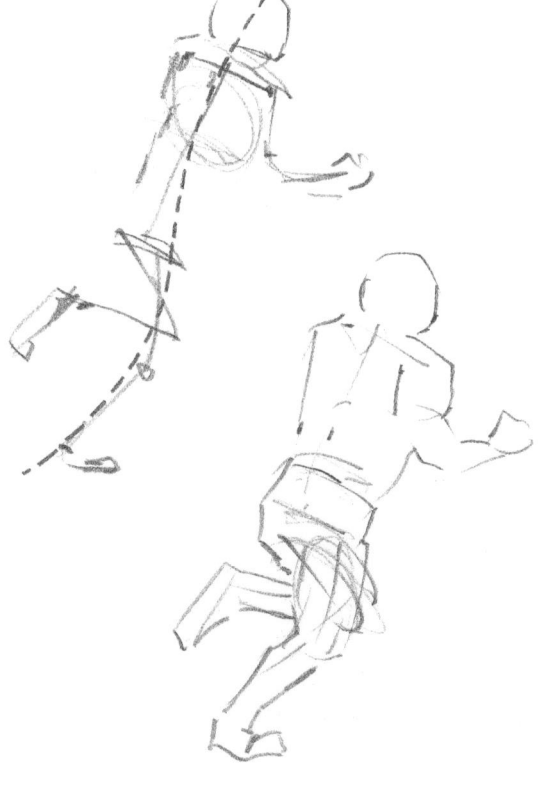

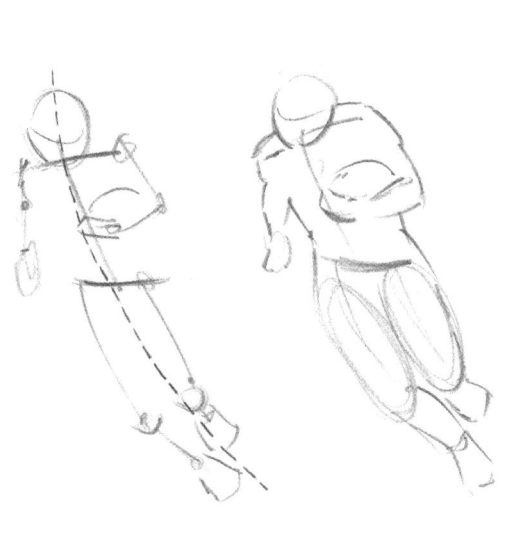

Working Quickly To capture the action accurately, work very quickly, without including even a suggestion of detail. If you want to correct a line, don't stop to erase, just draw over it.

Once you compile a series of gesture drawings, you can combine them into a scene of people in action.

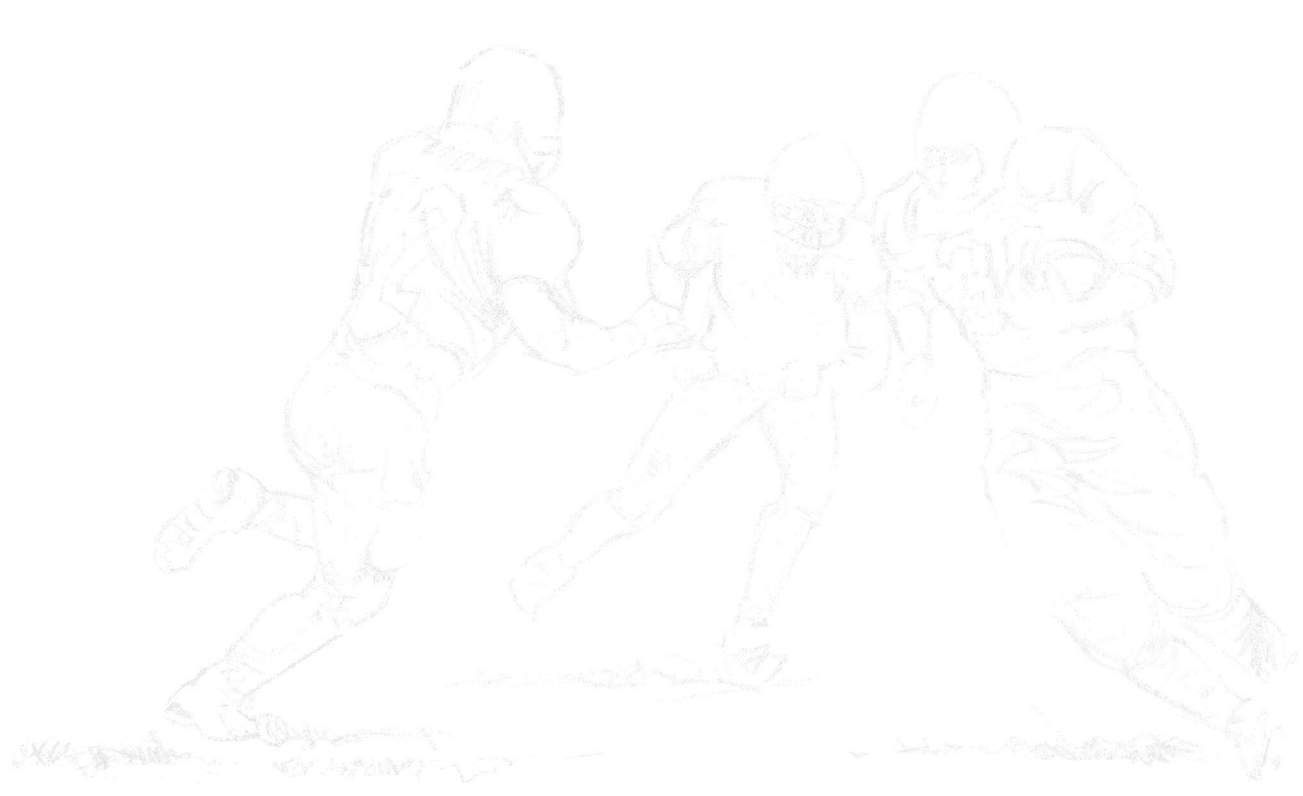

Graceful Movement

Before drawing this ballerina, lightly sketch the centerline of balance as well as the line of action representing the shape of her spine. Start out with straight lines to lay out her body parts in correct proportion, eventually smoothing out the lines in accordance with her body contours.

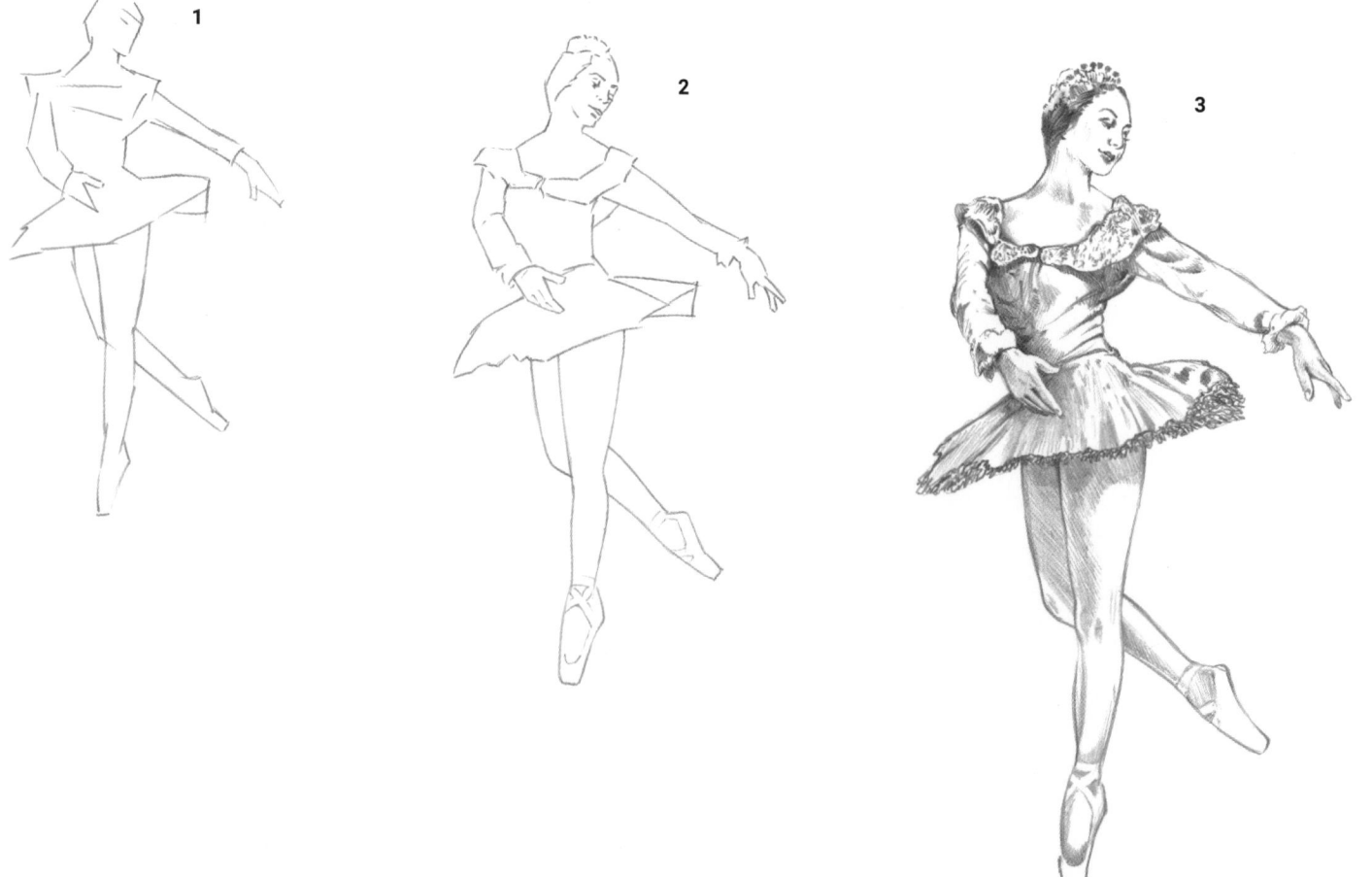

Fill in the figure below, taking note of small details such as the folds in her costume and the position of her fingers.

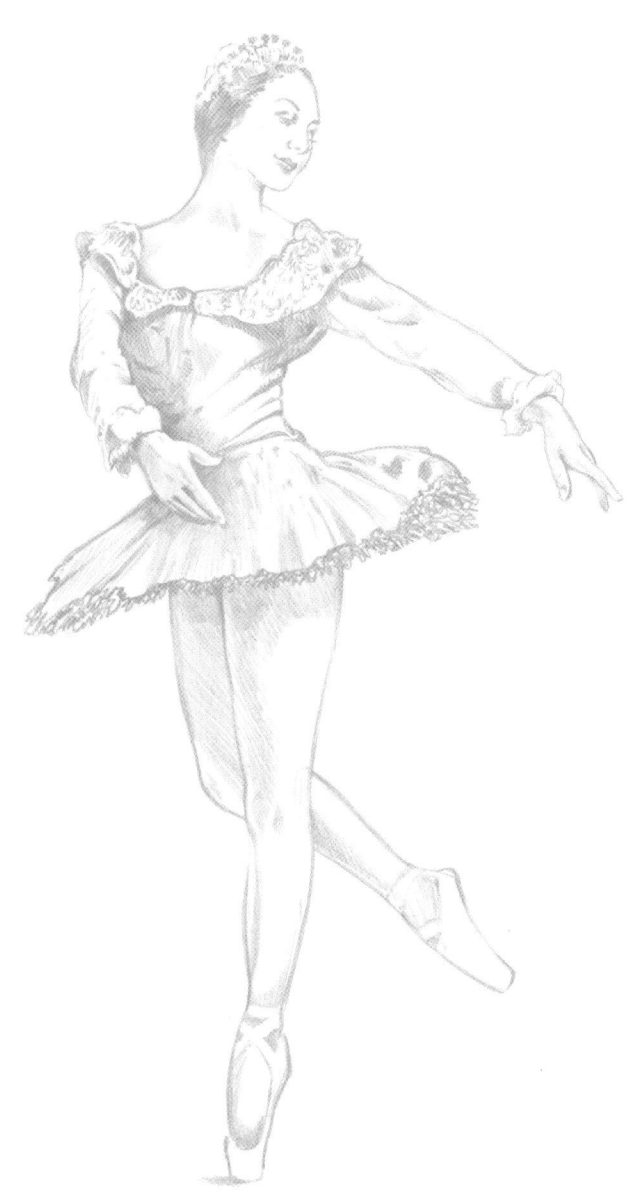

Blocking in Shadows

To keep the feeling of free movement, don't draw perfectly refined lines and shadows. Instead, focus on making delicate outlines for the dancers, and quickly lay in broad, dark strokes for their clothing.

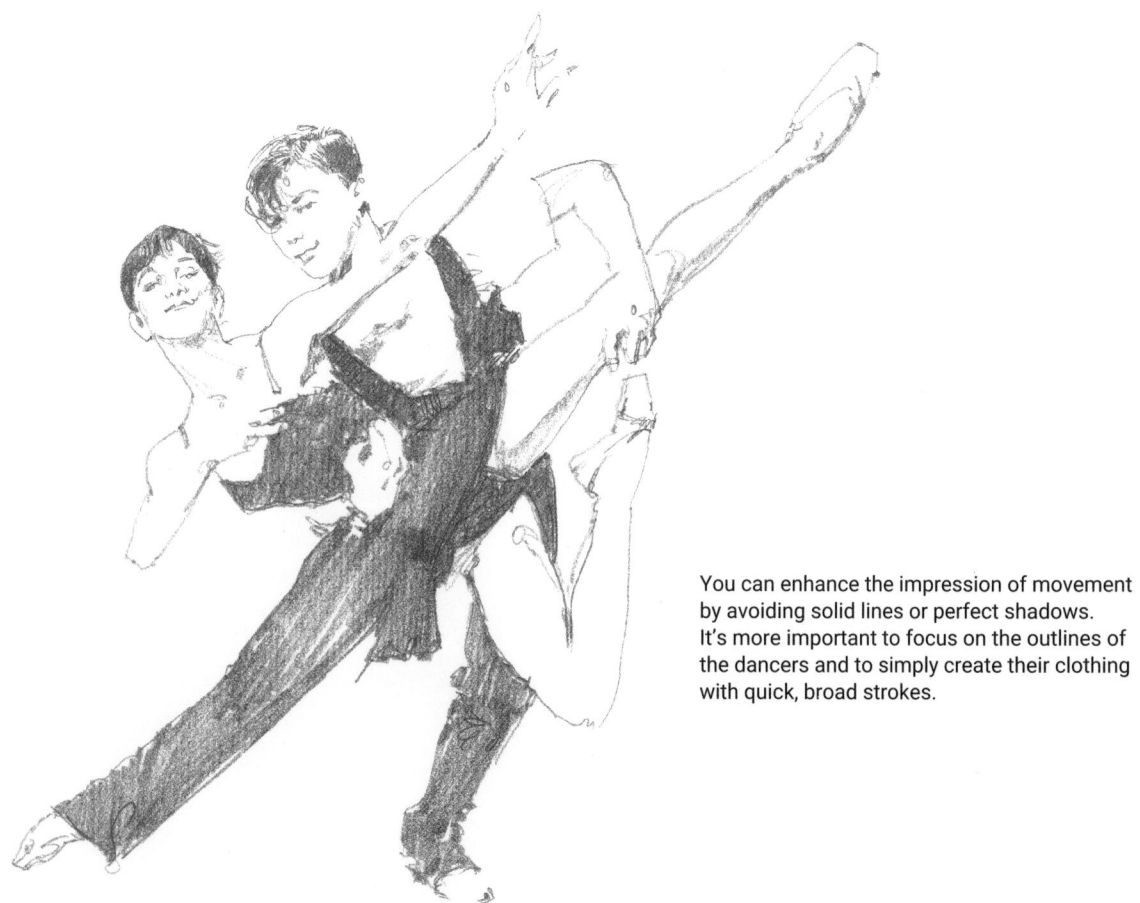

You can enhance the impression of movement by avoiding solid lines or perfect shadows. It's more important to focus on the outlines of the dancers and to simply create their clothing with quick, broad strokes.

Using all the skills you have learned,
complete the drawing using the outline below.

Bending and Twisting

When people are actively moving, they bend and twist their bodies. Clothing helps convey the appearance of a twisting body through the folds. Keep in mind that folds on a twisting body will be tighter than folds on a person in a still pose.

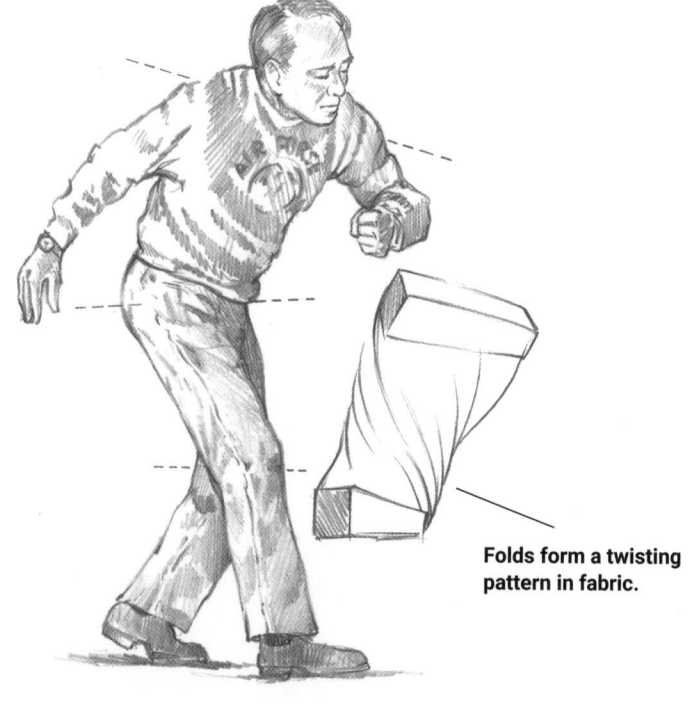

Folds form a twisting pattern in fabric.

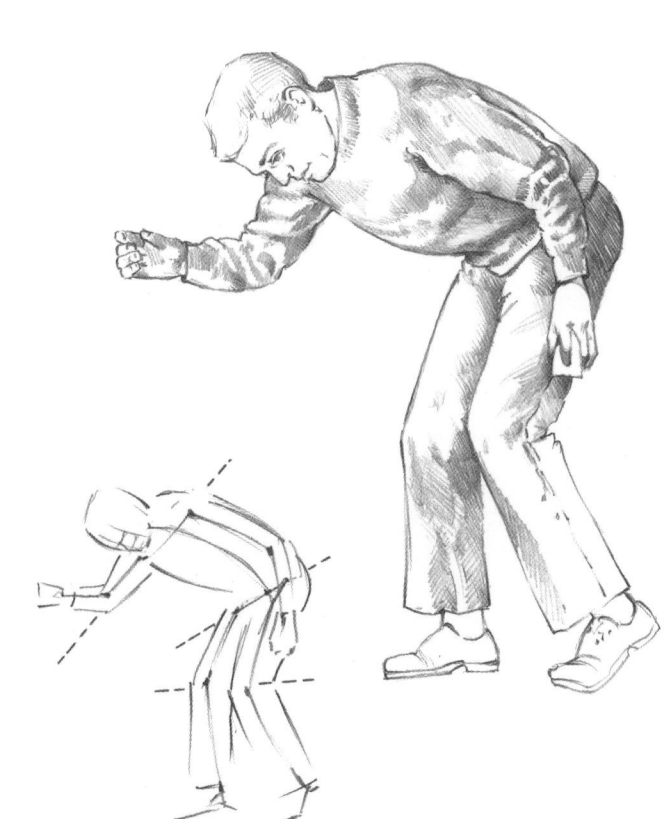

Finish drawing the clothing on the figure below. Add shading to show realistic folds in the garments where the body is twisting.

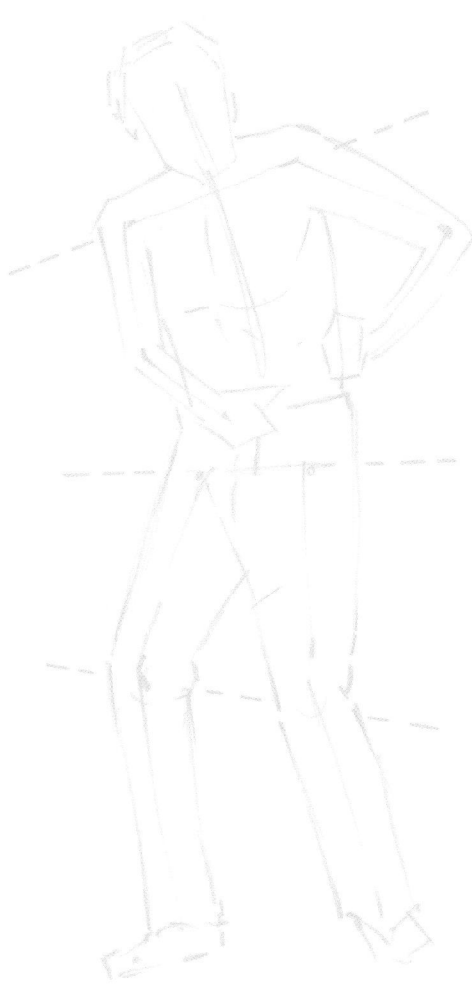

Realistic Depictions

In almost every position, all parts of the body work together to maintain balance. The flexibility of the joints, muscles, and tendons allows humans to perform extremely complex movements. To correctly draw bending and stretching, for example, take a look at these examples. Pay attention to the fit of the clothing—and especially the folds.

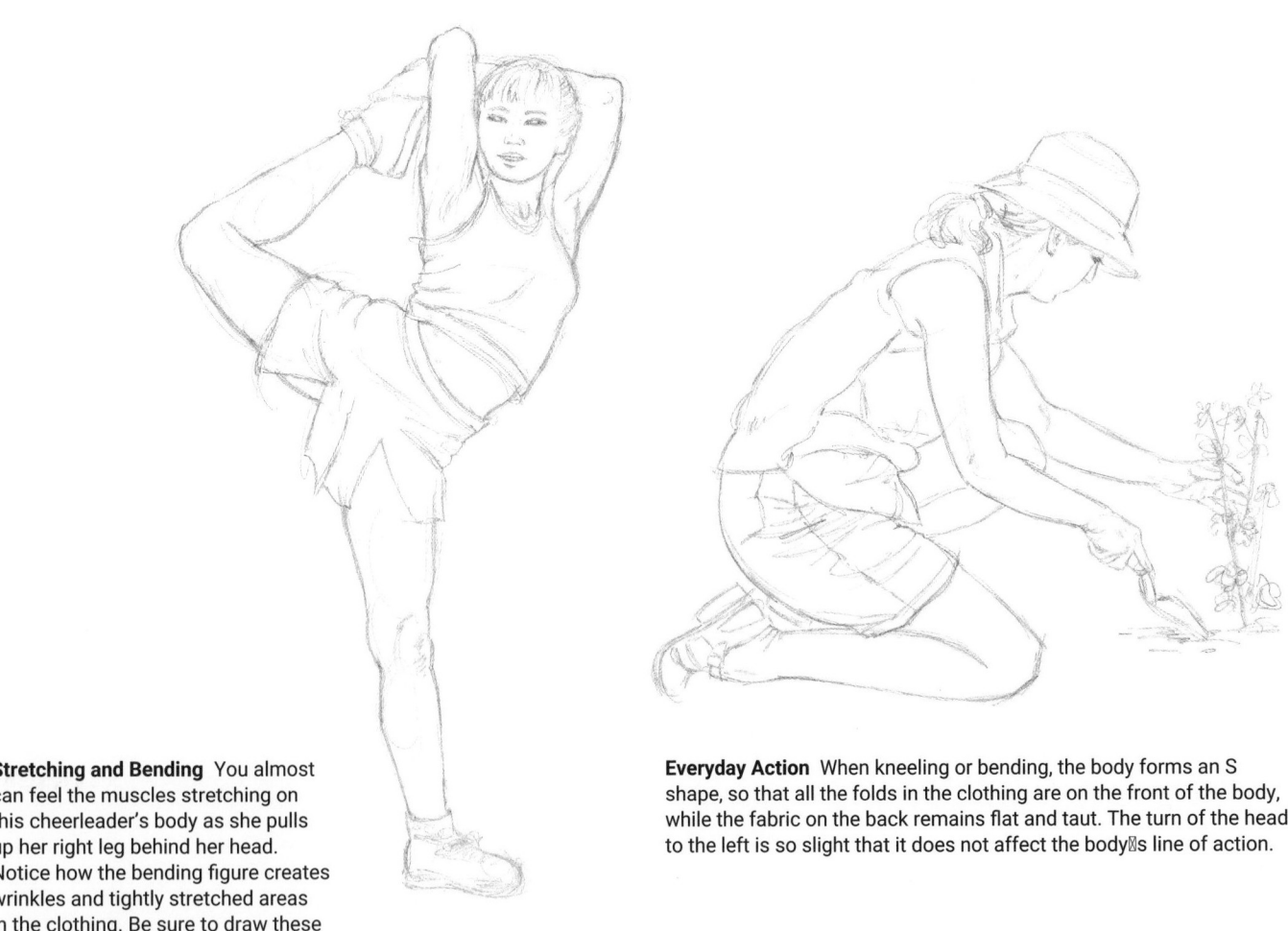

Stretching and Bending You almost can feel the muscles stretching on this cheerleader's body as she pulls up her right leg behind her head. Notice how the bending figure creates wrinkles and tightly stretched areas in the clothing. Be sure to draw these creases and smooth areas to make your drawing believable.

Everyday Action When kneeling or bending, the body forms an S shape, so that all the folds in the clothing are on the front of the body, while the fabric on the back remains flat and taut. The turn of the head to the left is so slight that it does not affect the body's line of action.

Practice drawing the body in movement poses using the outlines below.

Drawing Clothing

As your skills improve, techniques become important for making your depictions more vibrant and realistic. Properly depicting clothing is a key factor in this.

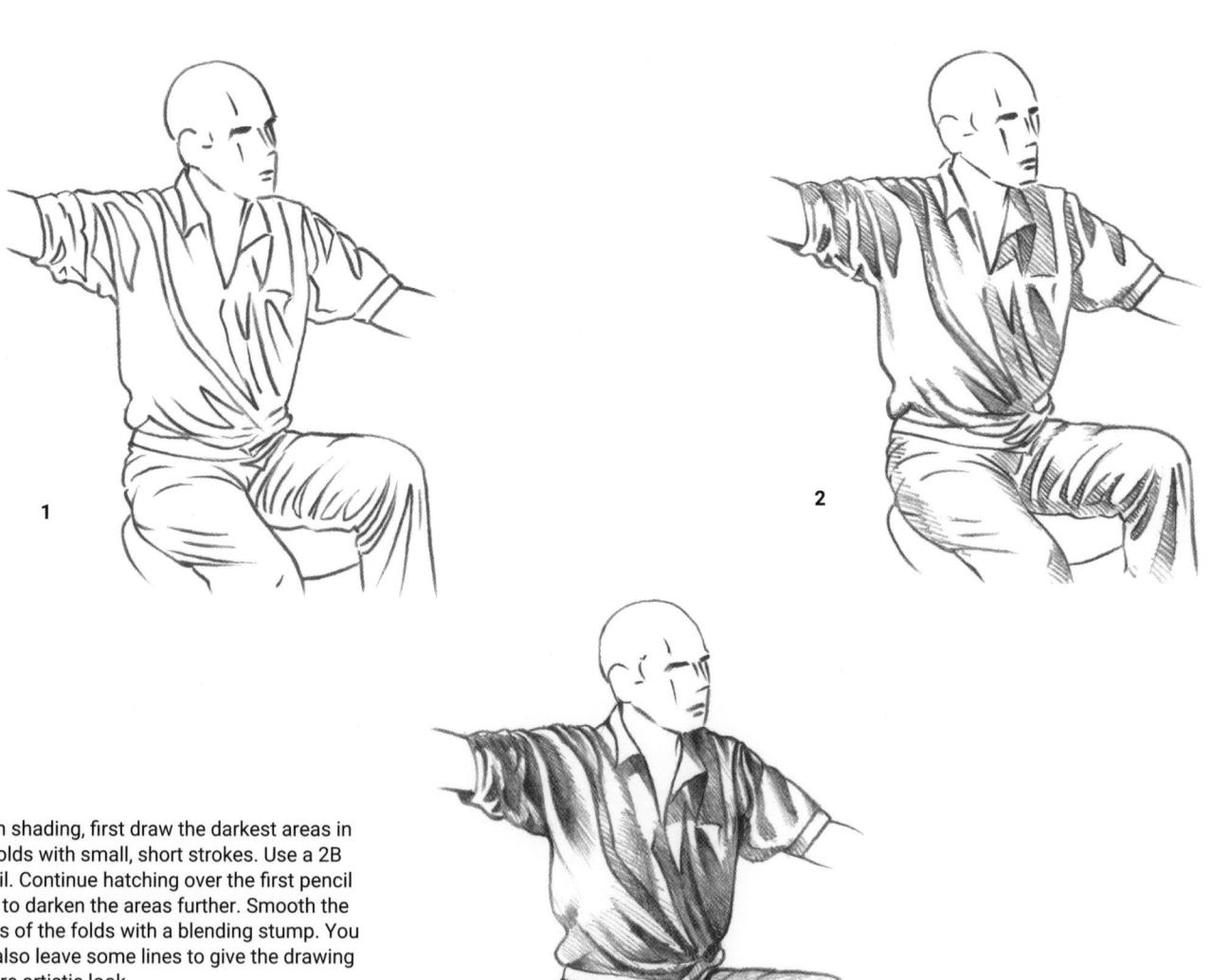

When shading, first draw the darkest areas in the folds with small, short strokes. Use a 2B pencil. Continue hatching over the first pencil lines to darken the areas further. Smooth the edges of the folds with a blending stump. You can also leave some lines to give the drawing a more artistic look.

Roughly sketch the clothing with initial construction lines for the folds; these will help guide the shading as you complete the drawing.

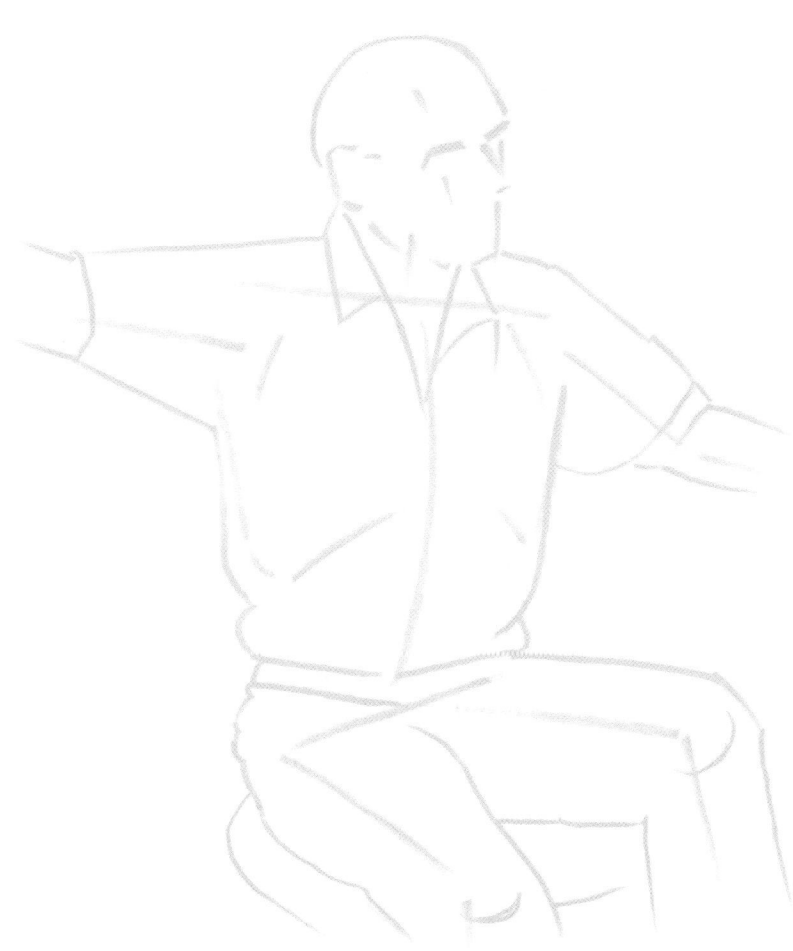

Foreshortening

Foreshortening refers to the visual effect (or optical illusion) that an object is shorter than it actually is because it is angled toward the viewer. Objects or people closer to the viewer appear proportionately larger than objects farther away. Foreshortening helps create a three-dimensional effect and can provide dramatic emphasis. Study the following examples to see how foreshortening influences their sense of depth.

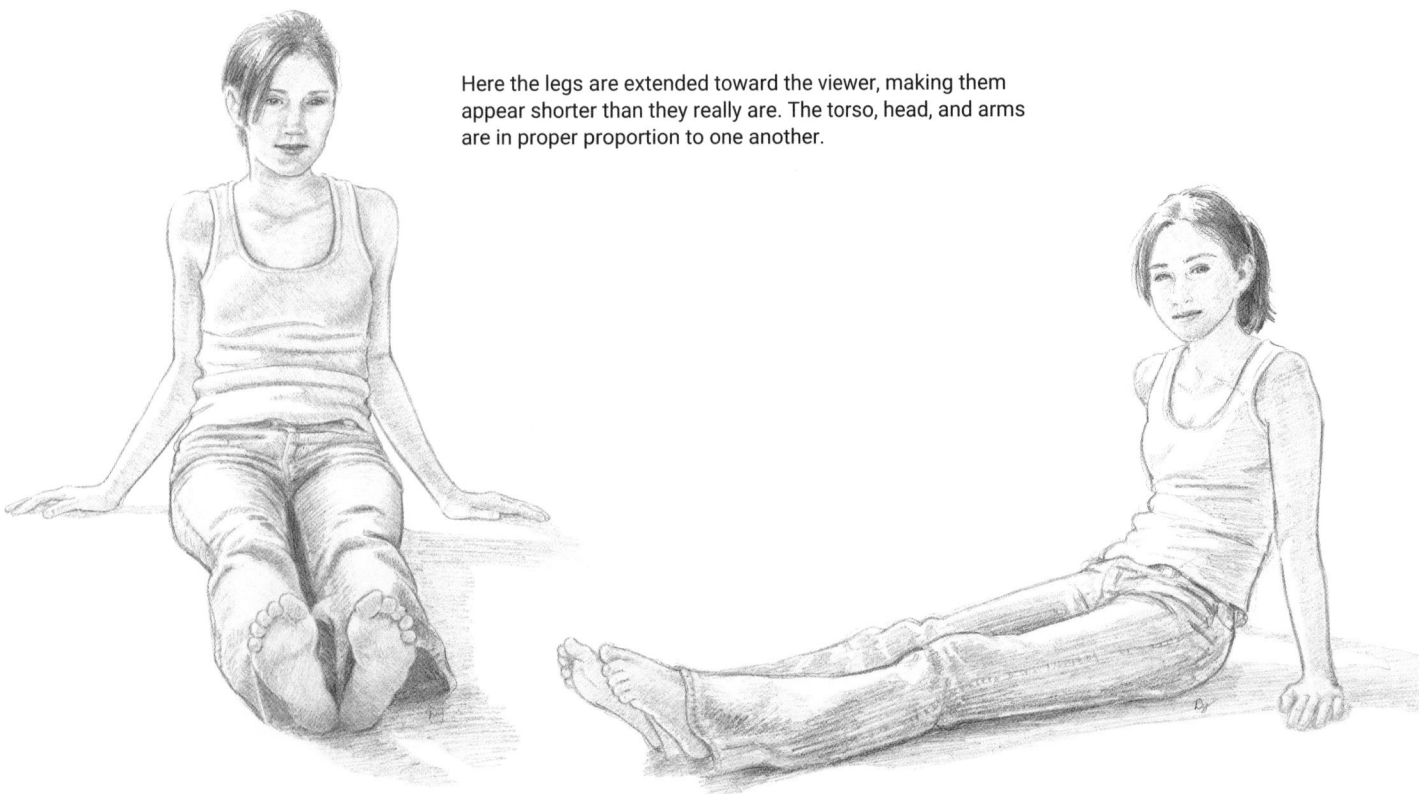

Here the legs are extended toward the viewer, making them appear shorter than they really are. The torso, head, and arms are in proper proportion to one another.

In this view, the limbs are not distorted because the view is directly from the side. The torso, head, and legs are roughly the same distance from the viewer. The fingers of the left hand are somewhat foreshortened.

In this view, most of the body is on the same plane (and parallel to the picture plane), but the head and arms are angled slightly away from the viewer and appear relatively small when compared with the rest of the body.

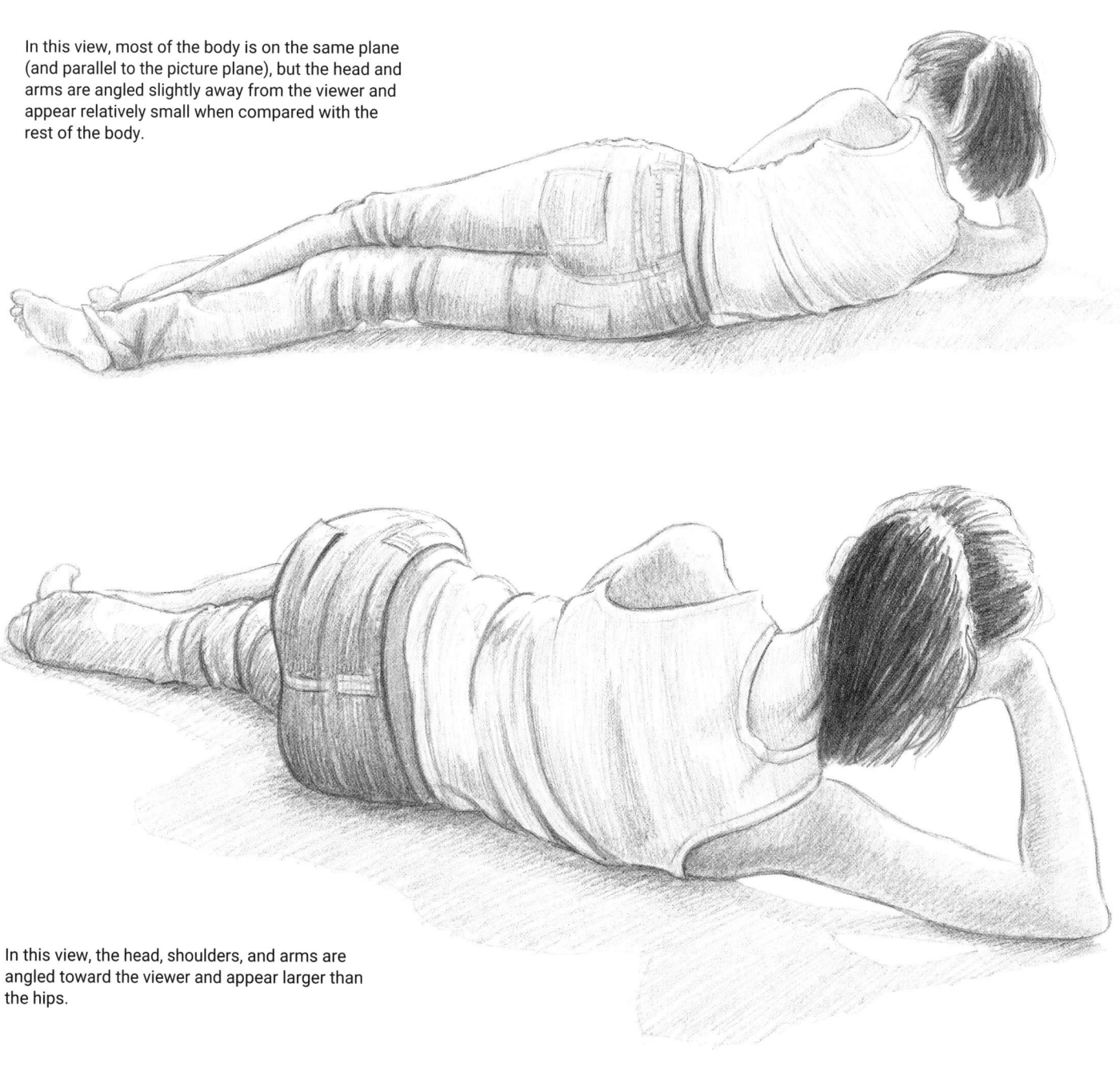

In this view, the head, shoulders, and arms are angled toward the viewer and appear larger than the hips.

Reclining Figure

Put your newfound foreshortening skills to use. First, study the photograph.
Then sketch the figure on a paper, or trace the outline on the next page.

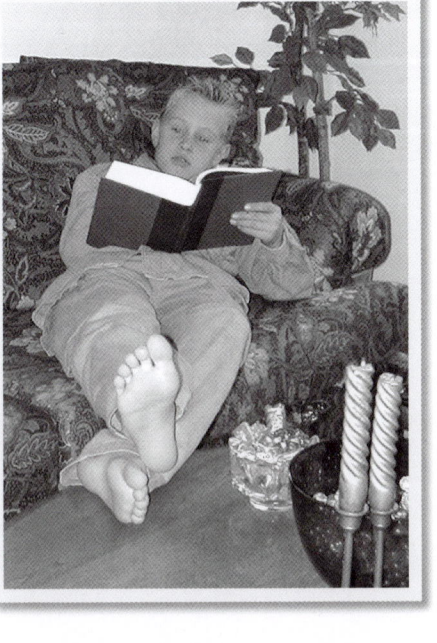

This photo is an excellent example of optical foreshortening. Do you see how the feet look larger than the head? Of course, in reality, the viewer's legs are longer than they appear, and the head is not as small as it seems in the photograph. But the angle from which the photo was taken creates a foreshortened effect.

Start with short, quick strokes to sketch an outline of the subject, paying attention to the spatial depth of the photograph.

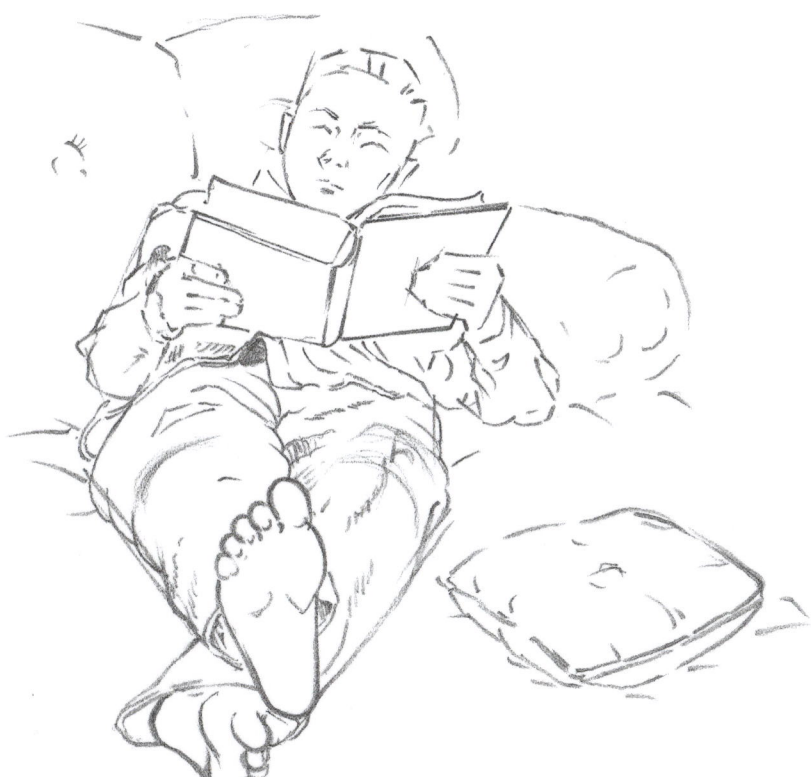

Trace the drawing below to clearly see the foreshortening.
Add shading using light hatching strokes. For an added challenge,
use a fineline marker to complete the drawing.

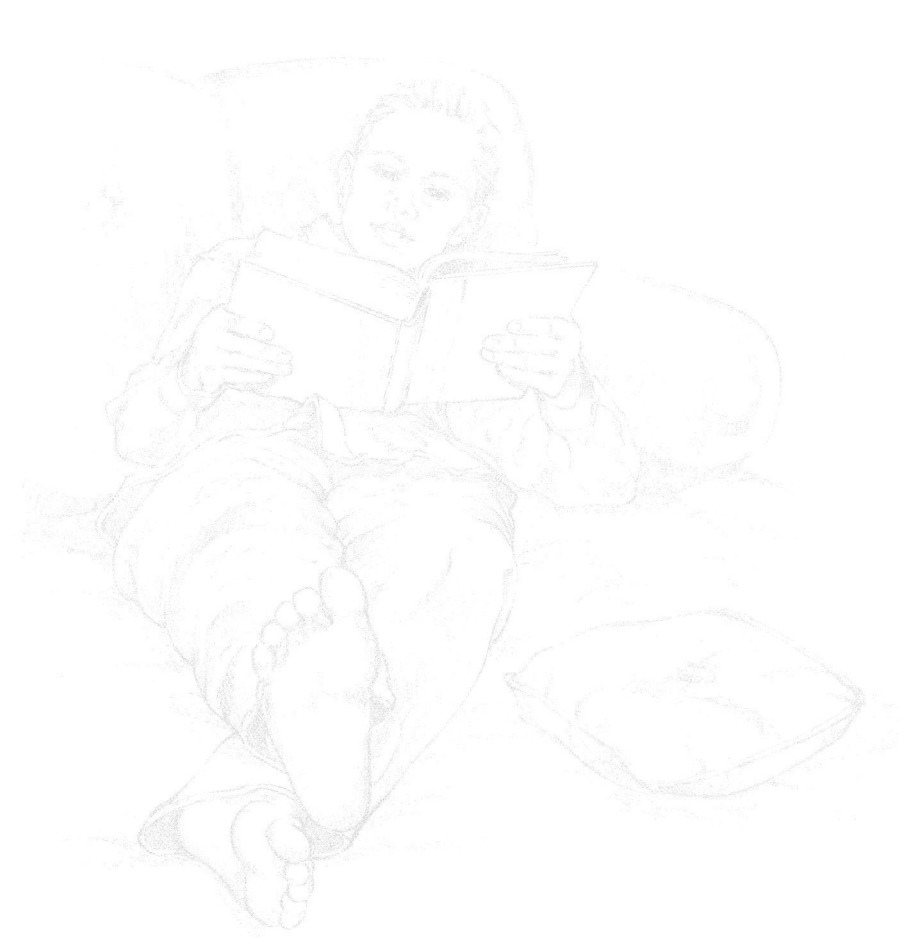

Drawing from Life

Drawing from life (or drawing from a live model) is a wonderful exercise for beginners. It prevents you from overworking your drawing because you're focused on quickly recording the details of your model(s) before they move. Because you're working at a faster pace, drawing from life will help you learn freedom and flexibility—both of which will benefit your drawings. It will also help you appreciate the subtleties the eye perceives that the camera can't, such as the twinkle in this model's eye.

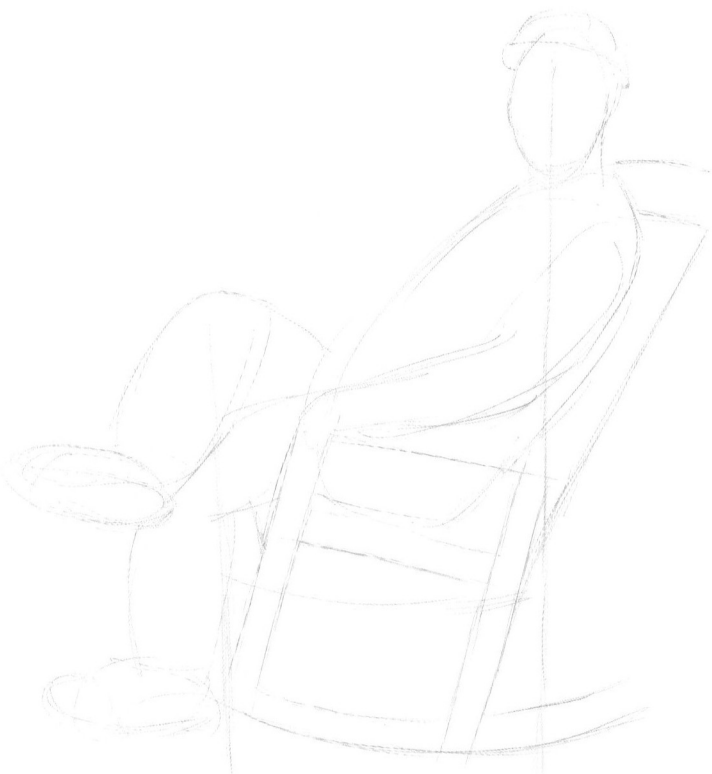

1 Using an HB pencil, lightly block in the basic shapes of the figure and the rocking chair. Foreshorten the right leg and make the right foot larger.

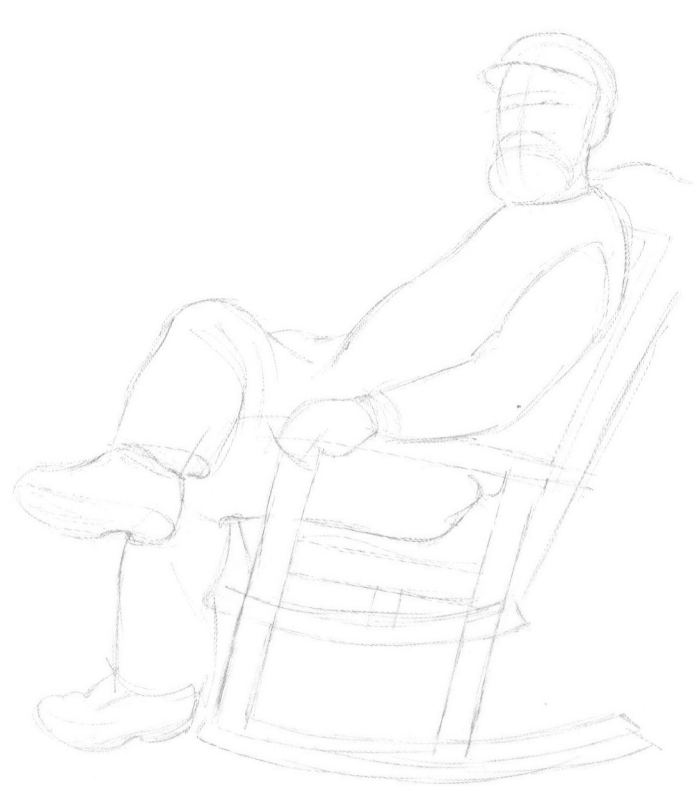

2 Begin to refine the shapes, indicating the clothing and shoes. Then block in the mustache and beard, and place guidelines for the facial features.

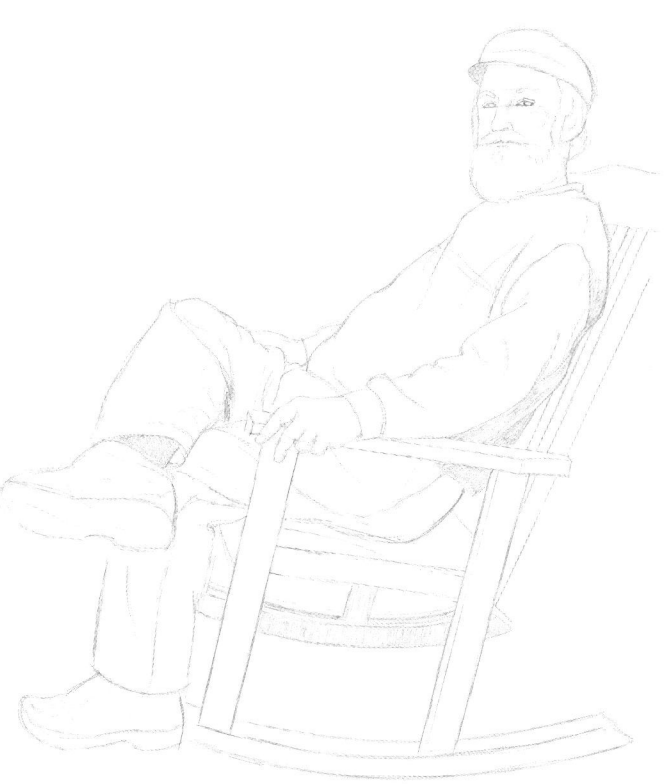

3 With a B pencil, draw in the facial features and refine the shapes of the head, including the ear, hair, and hat. Refine the rest of the body, and continue to develop the chair.

4 Using a 2B pencil, shade the hat and clothing. Add some detailing to the hair and beard with short strokes, following the direction of growth. Continue to refine your drawing.

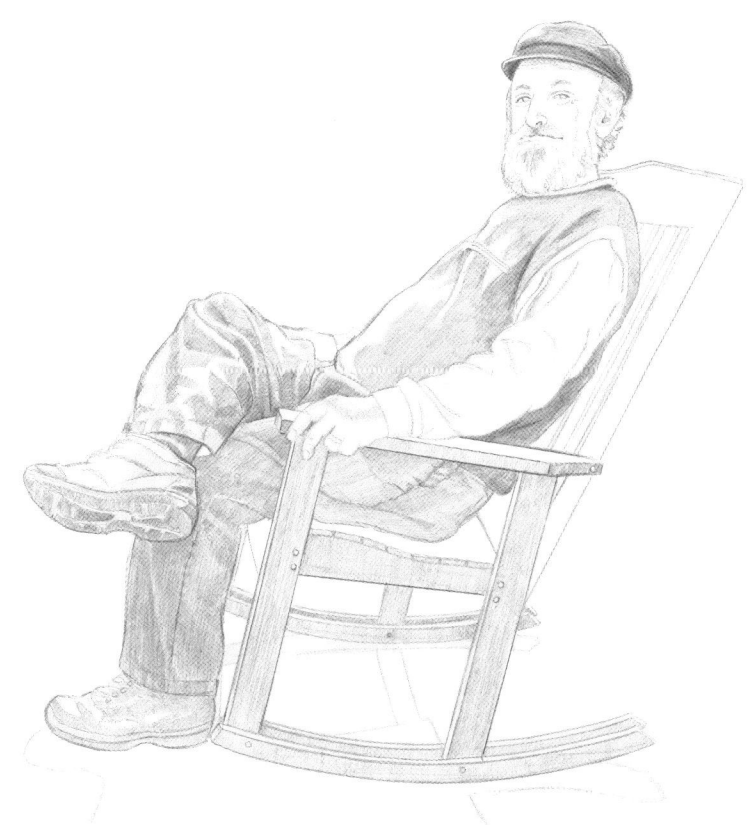

Face Detail

To create the beard, apply dark tones to areas of the beard, showing the gaps between groups of hair. Leave some areas of the paper white to reflect where the beard is in sunlight. Shade lightly to indicate wrinkles and creases, which should appear soft. Use a kneaded eraser to lift out a highlight in the eye.

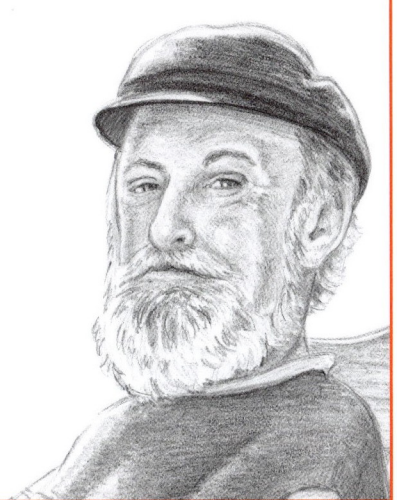

5 Add shading to the eyes, nose, mouth, ear, hair, and facial hair. Shade the clothing and chair, adjusting the lights and shadows as needed. Use a 4B pencil for the darkest areas. Soften any hard edges with an eraser or a blending stump.

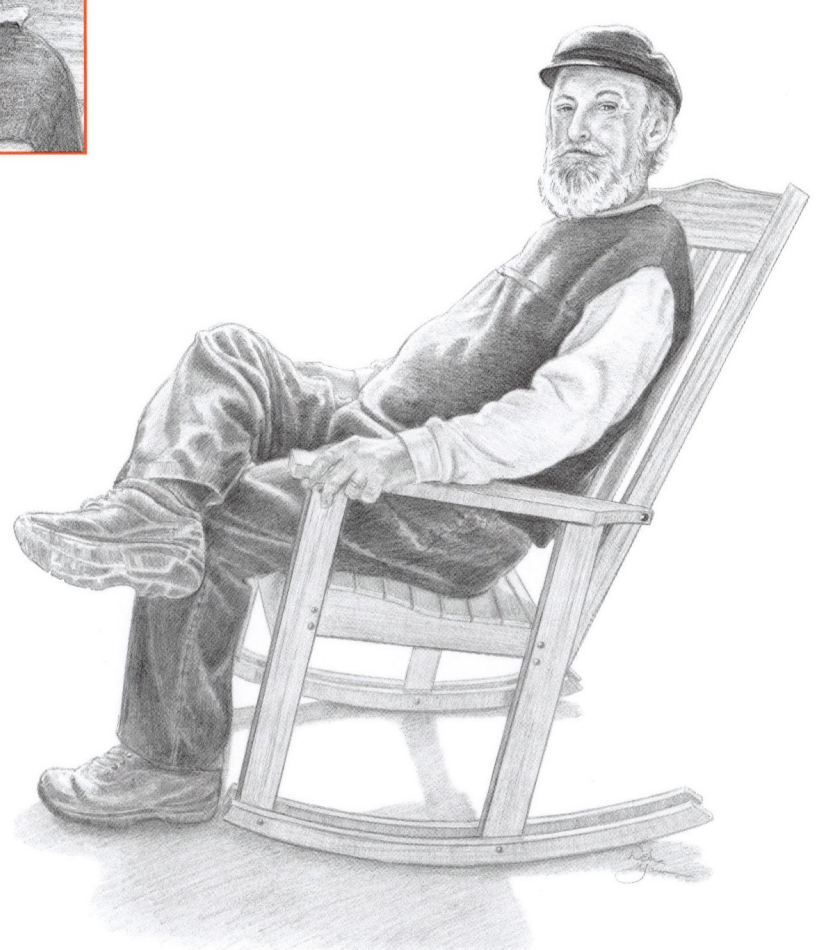

Finish the outline below to master the various techniques you've learned up to this point, including foreshortening, facial features, clothing folds, and dynamic poses.

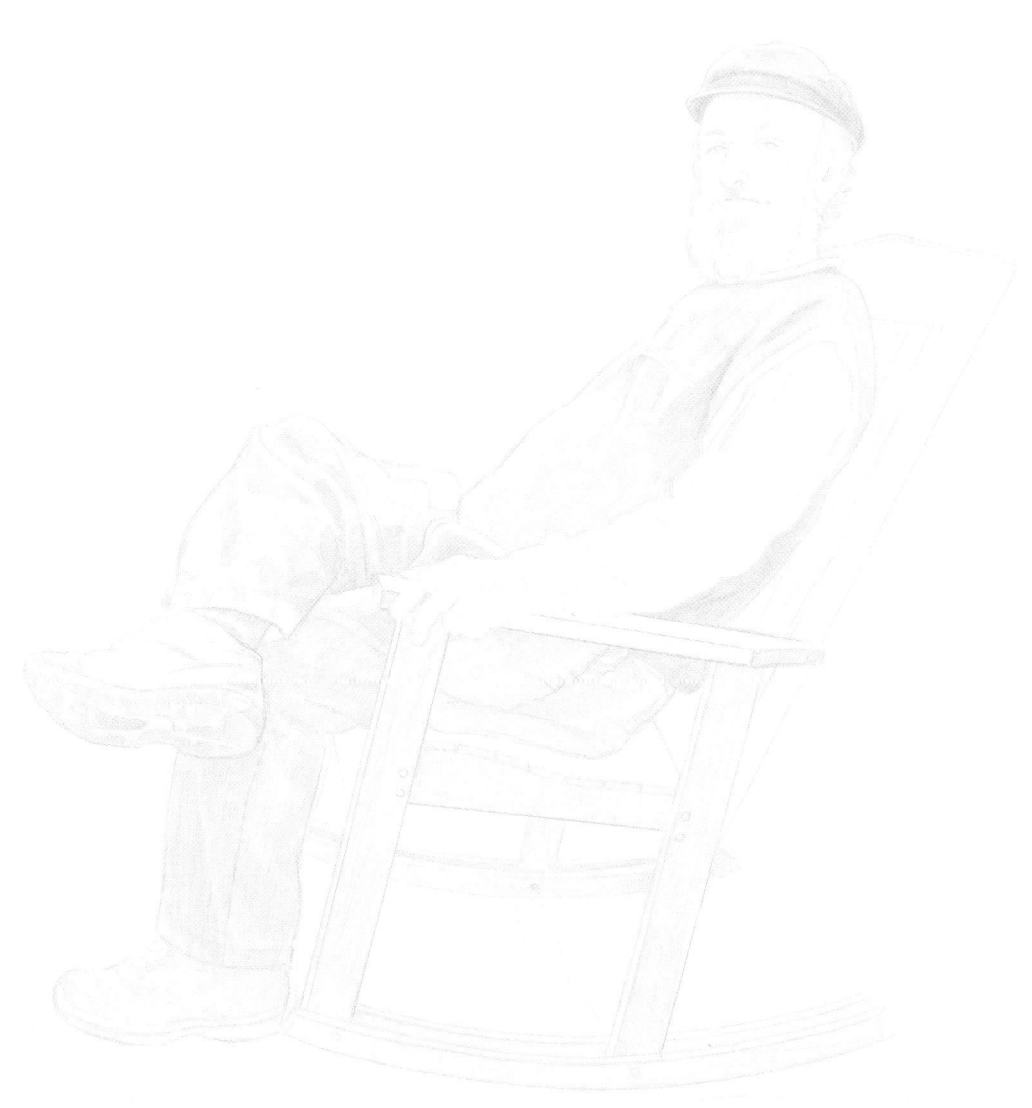

Quarto.com
WalterFoster.com

© 2026 Quarto Publishing
Artwork on back cover (face, hand, and young woman) and pages 1, 3, 23–25, 28–34, 36–41, 44–58, 62–63, 69–70, 75, 78–79, 82–87, 100–103, 116–117, 120–121, 124–127 © 2006, 2007, 2009 Debra Kauffman Yaun; pages 2, 4–9, 13 (sphere) © 2005 Walter Foster Publishing; pages 10, 80–81 © 1997, 2003, 2006 Diane Cardaci; back cover (ballerina) and pages 12, 14–17, 20–22, 26–27, 42–43, 66–68, 71–74, 90–99, 104–105, 108–111, 114–115, 118–119, 122–123 © 1989, 1997, 2001, 2003, 2004, 2005, 2009 William F. Powell; back cover (figure) and pages 13 (cone), 65, 88, 106–107, 112–113 © 1999, 2003, 2005, 2009 Michael Butkus; front cover (girl) and pages 18–19, 76–77 © 2011 Nathan Rohlander; pages 60–61, 64 © 2004, 2005, 2009 Ken Goldman.

First published in 2026 by Walter Foster Publishing, an imprint of The Quarto Group,
100 Cummings Center, Suite 265-D, Beverly, MA 01915, USA.
T (978) 282-9590 F (978) 283-2742

EEA Representation, WTS Tax d.o.o.,
Žanova ulica 3, 4000 Kranj, Slovenia.
www.wts-tax.si

Walter Foster Publishing titles are also available at discount for retail, wholesale, promotional, and bulk purchase. For details, contact the Special Sales Manager by email at specialsales@quarto.com or by mail at The Quarto Group, Attn: Special Sales Manager, 100 Cummings Center, Suite 265-D, Beverly, MA 01915, USA.

30 29 28 27 26   1 2 3 4 5

ISBN: 978-1-57715-737-3

Digital edition published in 2026
eISBN: 978-1-57715-738-0

Produced by Coffee Cup Creative LLC
Layout by Debbie Aiken
Proofread by Stephanie Carbajal

Printed in Guangdong, China TT122025

Featured Artists

Michael Butkus ▪ Diane Cardaci
William F. Powell ▪ Ken Goldman
Nathan Rohlander ▪ Debra Kauffman Yaun